THIS IS MAGIC

This is Magic

SECRETS OF THE CONJURER'S CRAFT

by

WILL DEXTER

BELL PUBLISHING COMPANY · NEW YORK

CONTENTS

A WORD FROM THE PUBLISHERS

A YEAR OR MORE ago we asked Mr. Will Dexter to write for us a history of the conjurer's art. He said he'd be delighted to do so. The manuscript should be ready, he thought, in something like twenty or thirty years' time, with any luck.

He went on to suggest, with growing enthusiasm, that we should discuss the expenses likely to be incurred. There would be, he murmured with rapture, visits to New York, Paris, and Vienna. Library research had to be done there, he explained. And he was sure we would appreciate the necessity of fairly long sojourns in India, Pakistan, and whatever portions of China and Egypt were available to him. Field research was the term he applied to those remote pastures.

Would we, he asked, prefer to make him an annual allowance to cover these projects, or should he send us a monthly statement of expenses? After the first few years, he thought, the arrangements should be working smoothly, and several volumes of the work might have been completed.

When would we like him to start for New York? Next month? Next week? Tomorrow?

Regretfully, we stemmed Mr. Dexter's enthusiasm. We couldn't wait twenty or thirty years for the manuscript, we explained. We were appalled at the vast expenses he hinted at. We didn't want a work of ten or twelve volumes. All we wanted (and at this stage we may have banged the desk a little to enforce the point) was a book. *A* book, in the singular. And we wanted it within a year.

When Mr. Dexter had finished telling us just why it would be impossible to write a history of magic in one year, or contain it in one volume, we modified our request a little. Then let it be, we suggested, a condensed history. Let it be the story of this trick or that trick. For example, we added (and here we began to become enthusiastic ourselves), what was the oldest conjuring trick in the world? What was the

newest? Were the Piddingtons really telepathic? How does
a magician saw a girl in half? Do conjurers use marked cards?
How do they do the Indian Rope Trick?

Mr. Dexter went away thoughtfully. A year later, to the
day, he brought us the manuscript of this book. We read it.
We liked it. We read it again. We liked it even more.

So will you.

THIS IS MAGIC

Chapter One

THE SECRET FROM THE TOMB

IN THE GREAT stone palace at Memphis, beside the Nile, Khufu, King of All Egypt and Lord of the Three Worlds, nods his head and raises his hand. In answer to the signal, the leather-armoured guards at the door fling open the heavy wooden portals. From somewhere remotely outside comes the strident blast of a trumpet, echoing eerily down the dim, dark corridors.

And then—silence. A silence broken gradually by the soft pad of sandalled feet. An awesome silence, not easy for the stiff-standing courtiers to bear.

Up the long passage to the doors of the throne room walks a man, striding his slow way between the lines of burly Nubians guarding the entrance. An old man, he is, but one who bears about him all the marks of dignity.

The guards stand motionless, only their eyes, widely white in the shining ebony of their faces, telling of the fear they feel in the presence of this man.

For this is Dedi, the Magician, a legend among men, a familiar of the gods, a sorcerer with all the powers of Hell at his command.

He has lived for one hundred and ten years, men say. He has proclaimed that he can never die, they say. For food, he eats five hundred loaves and a shoulder of beef every day, they say. His daily drink is one hundred flagons of beer, they say.

He is a magician, they say.

In royal state Dedi has been brought from the town of Ded-Snefru by Gardadathu, son of Khufu, at the Pharaoh's command. Command? Rather say, request, for Khufu, as much as any man, respects the wizard's reputation. And Khufu has a favour to ask of this aged sorcerer.

1

Dedi has let it be known that he alone can advise the Pharaoh as to where can be found the marble and alabaster, the onyx and the basalt, that will be needed for the Temple of Thoth, the majestic shrine which Khufu is building near the Great Pyramid destined for his tomb.

Dedi pauses by the doors of the throne room, and slowly inclines his head to the Pharaoh. The gesture is returned, and then, unbidden, the wizard slowly paces the length of the long chamber until he stands before the steps of the dais.

Khufu speaks. "I am told, Dedi, that thou art a magician?"

Dedi bows assent.

"Men speak of thy power to reunite heads severed from their bodies," Khufu continues, repeating one of the many legends associated with the powers of Dedi.

"That I can do, great King," acknowledges the wizard.

The Pharaoh waves his hand to a courtier. "Let a criminal be brought here," he commands.

Dedi halts the courtier. "Great King," he says, "my power does not extend to men. I can resurrect only animals."

A goose is brought. Dedi draws a knife from beneath his robe, and with one stroke severs its head, which he holds out on his open palm for all to see. The bird lies, headless, before the throne of Khufu.

The magician stoops, lays the head against the neck, and the goose stand up, shakes itself, and waddles away.

Dedi performs the same miracle with other birds, and at last, as the crowning effect, upon a live bull calf. Each time the creatures are restored to full life.

Is this magic?

What else?

And so men talked of the powers of Dedi long after the wizard had disappeared from human sight. From generation to generation in the palaces beside the Nile the story was told. Dedi, the sorcerer who could restore life to a headless animal. Dedi, they said, who could make the lions of the desert follow him like the tame cats about the temples. Dedi, who would live for ever. Was Dedi really dead.. . .?

Dead or not, he lived as a legend, and a potent legend, for his fame passed from generation to generation by word

of mouth. It was not until a thousand years after his Royal
Command Performance for Khufu—better known today as
Cheops, builder of the Great Pyramid—that the story of his
powers was put into words and written down.

It was an anonymous scribe who penned the tale, nearly
4,000 years ago, which makes Dedi's Cut and Restored Goose
illusion something like 5,000 years old. You'll find the story
in various translations of what has become known as the Westcar Papyrus—the first written account of a conjuring trick,
the experts say.

There's even a mystery about the papyrus itself. It's believed
to have been recovered from an ancient Egyptian tomb about
150 years ago. An Egyptologist named Henry Westcar, visiting
Egypt in 1823, acquired the papyrus, which afterwards came
into the possession of Karl Richard Lepsius, who died in 1884.
After his death, the manuscript passed to the Berlin State
Museum, and its presence there was known up to 1939.

Then came the war. The Berlin State Museum authorities
now declare that the papyrus "is not, as a result of the after-
math of war, in Berlin at the present time."

Magician Peter Warlock, who has made considerable investigations into the papyrus and its story, says that informed
opinion in London believes that all papyri from Berlin were
carried off to Moscow during the Russian occupation.

"But," he writes in *The Magic Circular,* organ of the Magic
Circle, "British sources in the Russian capital are not aware
of the Westcar Papyrus's being exhibited, or of the Soviet
Government's having admitted possession."

There are several translations of the Westcar Papyrus in
existence. All vary more or less in interpretation, but all agree
that Dedi apparently beheaded birds and a bull, restoring their
heads and their lives after the decapitation.

How was it done, this oldest recorded magical feat? More
to the point—*was* it done? You know how it is when someone tries to repeat the account of something he's seen. He
forgets. He exaggerates. He invents.

Is the story of the miracle performed before Cheops an
invention? Magicians believe it's a fairly true account of what
happened, and indeed may have been under-written, rather

than exaggerated. Today, five thousand years after Dedi stood before the Pharaoh, conjurers can make you believe that they have cut off a bird's head and restored it again. They can show you illusions in which an assistant's arm, leg, or head is severed from the body and replaced. They will even perform the illusion with volunteer members of the audience as "patients."

And what's the most famous illusion in the world today? Sawing a Woman in Half! Even Dedi had to confess that his power didn't extend to human subjects!

The trick of "decapitating" a bird is an easy one, but one that's rarely seen nowadays. In its most convincing form the conjurer has a sort of mitten, covered with feathers that match the bird's plumage. He also has a duplicate of the bird's head. The "mitten" is placed over the bird's head, the duplicate head is produced, and there's your trick.

Some conjurers use a bird whose head bends naturally back towards the body. Many pigeons will rest like this, with the head buried in the plumage of the back. Such a bird will hold its head among its feathers when placed in that position, so that you would swear the bird had no head.

I think Dedi's illusion with the bull calf was done by means of a piece of apparatus resembling the guillotine magicians today use for "amputating" their assistants' legs. In this, although it is first demonstrated that the blade passes through the hole where the leg is to be placed, a secret catch diverts the blade when the limb is in place, so that although the framework of the blade goes down, the blade doesn't.

Before we leave Dedi, it's interesting to note that even in translation the Westcar Papyrus has accumulated exaggerations. In some translations of the ancient document, the birds he beheaded are described as running across the floor to meet their decapitated heads, which ran to meet them and jumped into place on their necks!

Still, the wonder is that this 5,000-year-old trick hasn't been exaggerated even more than that. It would have been easier—and more impressive—for the Hyksos scribe of 4,000 years ago to make Dedi a *real* magician than for him to give a factual report of the performance.

Chapter Two

THE CUPS AND BALLS

IF EVER one conjuring trick above all others were to be nominated the standard test of a magician's skill it would be the ancient mystery of the Cups and Balls. The encyclopedic Professor Hoffmann, 19th century godfather of all today's books on magic, had this to say, in his thoughtful but wordy style, of the Cups and Balls: "It is, however, well worthy the attention of the student of modern magic, not only as affording an excellent course of training in digital dexterity, but as being, in the hands of an adept, most striking in effect. It is by no means uncommon to find spectators who have received more elaborate feats with comparative indifference, become interested, and even enthusiastic, over a brilliant manipulation of the Cups and Balls."

Professor Hoffmann was a master of the art of under-statement. Today's magical catalogues would say the same thing in four words: "This is a MUST!"

While we're quoting, let's go back a little further than Professor Hoffmann. This time, we have the written opinion of a gentleman who saw a conjurer at the theatre. This is what he wrote about the show: "One thing I remember, and I gape with astonishment at it now, and am almost struck dumb. A certain man stepped into the midst, and placed on a three-legged table three small cups, under which he concealed some little white round pebbles such as are found on the banks of rivers; these he placed one by one under the cups, and then—I don't know how—made them appear under another cup, and showed them in his mouth. That man is a most mysterious performer, and could beat Eurybates, of Oechalia, of whom we have heard."

That impressed spectator was one Athenaeus, writing from ancient Athens, for the Greeks had a word for the Cups and

5

Balls conjurer. *Psephopaikteo* they called him, and the name refers to the hiding of pebbles and making them appear in different places. The ancient Romans called the magicians who performed this trick *acetabularii*, from the Latin word for a cup. The ancient Egyptians no doubt also had a word for the magicians they portrayed so often, but the scholarship of the present writer does not extend as far as the Nilotic dialects. Nevertheless, the Cups and Balls was performed in ancient Egypt. It if wasn't, then the artists of that day were extraordinarily anticipatory in some of their papyri and tomb inscriptions, for you'll see pictures thereon of entertainers busily occupied with three cups and a ball.

In the Middle Ages, strolling jugglers used to show the Cups and Balls to the baffled yokels, and again, artists of the time preserved the picture for posterity. Hieronymus Bosch, who died in 1516, painted a famous picture of a magician performing the Cups and Balls trick to an admiring throng. Incidentally, he shows the conjurer's confederate busily lifting a spectator's purse. Conjurers were maligned, even in those days.

The first book to teach conjuring tricks—*The Anatomie of Legerdemain, by Hocus Pocus Junior*—published more than 300 years ago, had an explanatory picture which might almost have been taken from a present-day book of tricks.

There are some learned writers on magic who claim that one of the French names for conjuring—*escamoterie*—is taken from *escamote*, meaning a juggler's cork ball. But it's far more likely that an *escamote* was so called because it was used by an *escamoteur*.

After that little excursion into the past, let's get down to the trick itself. What *is* this Cups and Balls trick?

If you haven't seen it (which would be a surprising thing) the plot is easy to explain. It's the same plot that baffled Athenaeus, the same trick illustrated by the 17th century artist in *Hocus Pocus Junior*, the same routine that magicians present today, and will no doubt be presenting in another thousand years' time.

The magician has three empty cups. Under one of them he places a small ball. He lifts another cup, and the ball is seen

to have travelled from cup number one to that one. A duplicate ball, you say? No it isn't. Look. Here's cup number one.
And there's no ball under it. Where is the ball? Under cup
number two? Of course not. You weren't watching. It's here
—under cup number three.

And so it goes on. From cup to cup dodges the little ball,
and you can never find it.

That sounds familiar to you? Of course it does. If you've
never seen the Cups and Balls Trick, at least you've heard of

THE CUPS AND BALLS

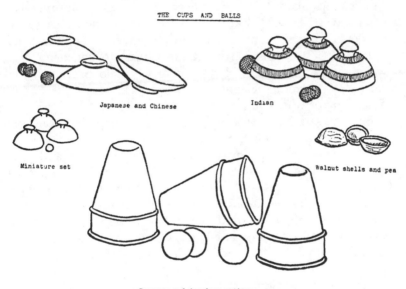

Japanese and Chinese   Indian

Miniature set   Walnut shells and pea

European and American pattern
Cups and Balls

its disreputable offspring, performed with three walnut shells
and a pea by furtive gentlemen on race-courses. Thimble-
rigging is a direct, if deplorable, grandchild of the ancient Cups
and Balls trick. The plot's the same, many of the secret moves
are the same, and the only thing that's different is the fact
that the spectator leaves the demonstration poorer than when
he went to it.

Within the last fifty years or so, the Cups and Balls trick
has extended side-shoots. Now, you may see the balls vanish,
change colour, become cubes, turn into live birds, or even
become glasses of whiskey. You may see the trick done with

one cup and several balls, or even without any cups, the balls being held in the magician's hand or in *your* hand. Sometimes, indeed, there are no cups and no balls. One version uses three matchboxes, one containing matches, and the others empty. The magician challenges the spectator to find the full box. And, of course, if we're to include all the one-in-three tricks, we might as well cite the infamous "Find the Lady" swindle.

Let's get back to a bit of honest deception.

The cups used by the magician are—nearly always—free from any trickery. So are the balls. It's all done, as you've no doubt guessed many a time, by the quickness of the hand.

Indeed, if we want a respectable witness to vouch for that, we've only to call upon His Worship Reginald Scot, J.P., that earnest 16th century Kentish magistrate who wrote the famous *Discouerie of Witchcraft*.

Scot wrote: "The true art, therefore, of juggling consisteth in legierdemain, to wit, the nimble conveiance of the hand, which is especiallie performed three waies. The first and principall consisteth in hiding and conveying of balles. . . . Concerning the ball, the plaies and devises thereof are infinite, in so much as if you can by use handle them well, you may showe therewith a hundred feats; but whether you seeme to throw the ball into your left hand, or into your mouth, or into a pot, or up into the aier, and it is to be kept still in your hand."

It's easy to imagine Scot being initiated into the mysteries of the Cups and Balls by some strolling juggler. And you don't have to read his "explanation" of the trick twice to realise that he was just as baffled at the end of his instructor's demonstration as he was at the beginning!

Scot didn't have much difficulty in persuading the conjurers of his time to show him how their tricks were done. His fellow magistrates had the habit of condemning conjurers to be burnt as witches, and it was Scot's researches into conjuring which proved that they were harmless entertainers. Mind you, he had difficulty putting across his views. Even after his book was written, you'd have had a long search before you could have bought a copy. Pretty well the whole of the first edition was burnt by the common hangman, on the instructions of King James, who *still* thought a magician was a witch!

If Scot thought about the Cups and Balls trick that "the plaies and devises thereof are infinite," what are we to think today, with all the new "plaies and devises"? New skills, new apparatus, new techniques, new methods of misdirection, make it seem even more akin to witchcraft!

If you'd really like to learn something of the skill needed to perform the Cups and Balls trick, try it for yourself. Buy three plastic beakers—the ones with a concave bottom and a slight ridge round the mouth are best. Make up a few small balls by cutting a rubber sponge into cubes and then trimming each to a round shape.

Ready? Then let's go ahead. Place the three beakers on the table, mouth downwards. Take a ball and pop it under beaker number one. There's a special way to do it. Lift the beaker with your right hand and place the ball, very openly and honestly, underneath it with the left hand. Now, as you lower the beaker over the ball, all you have to do is to take the ball out secretly without anyone seeing you do so!

This, you may think, is impossible. But it isn't. There are at least eight ways of taking the ball out with one hand as the cup is put down.

Now are you beginning to appreciate the skill that's needed for this most ancient of tricks?

Anyway, there's more to come. Your next job is to lift cup number two and show the ball—the same ball you've just taken from cup number one—lying on the table beneath cup number two.

More and more difficult, isn't it? But persevere. There are five ways of introducing a ball under a cup like this.

Now you have to make the ball vanish from cup number two and appear under cup number three.

And when you've mastered all this so that you can do it easily and successfully with people watching from all round you, we'll go on to another effect. This time, you'll use three balls, one under each cup, and by secretly stealing from one cup and loading under another, you'll finish up with all three balls under one cup.

It may be that after a few hours of struggling, you'll succeed in taking the ball out and popping it under—to *your* satisfaction. But will you be able to deceive other people as easily with your newly-learned secret moves? That's the test. Not easy, is it?

And believe me, many, many conjurers will agree with you. The Cups and Balls trick is too difficult even for them. It requires many weeks of steady practice, and after that many more weeks of constant rehearsal to perform correctly.

The basic moves are traditional among magicians, and there are many of them. I've outlined the elementary principle already—to take a ball secretly from one cup and place it secretly under another. Conjurers call this "stealing" and "loading."

Hundreds of books and articles have been written to teach conjurers the Cups and Balls trick, so it would be hopeless for me to attempt a full explanation of the secrets here—even if I were in full possession of all the secrets, and were prepared to disclose them. But here are one or two words of advice.

Firstly, the "steal." Try it this way. Place a ball on the table. Pick up a cup by grasping it at the mouth with thumb and forefinger. The other fingers will rest on the table as the cup is raised. Place the cup slowly over the ball, making sure that the front edge (the edge towards the audience) is slightly lower than the rear edge. As the front edge is about to touch the table, the free fingers come into play. The third finger and little finger swoop under the cup and grip the ball, carrying it into the palm of the hand. Then, without a break in the movement, the cup is placed down on the table.

This must be done slowly at first, to ensure smoothness of movement. Then, when you can pick up the cup, lower it, steal the ball, and complete the movement of placing the cup down—all in an unbroken sequence of smooth moves—then you can try to work a little faster.

A ball can be loaded under a cup by using the same movements in reverse. Or you might like to try another way of loading a ball. To do this, you must first have learned to hold a ball palmed. That's not difficult. Place a ball between the fleshy base of the thumb and the palm, and contract the thumb. This will grip the ball, which will be released when you relax the pressure of the thumb. Easy, but it still needs lots of practice.

However, if you can palm a ball, you're ready to load a cup like this: Pick up the cup as before, with the thumb and forefinger. Lift it clear of the table to show that there's no ball there. As you do so, let the cup swivel round so that its mouth is pointing upwards. It will pivot between the thumb and forefinger quite easily, and you should find that the mouth of the cup is directly below the palmed ball. Now relax the thumb presssure, and the ball will drop into the cup.

THE CUPS AND BALLS

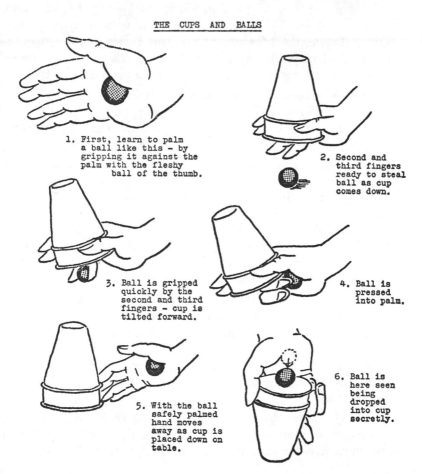

1. First, learn to palm a ball like this – by gripping it against the palm with the fleshy ball of the thumb.

2. Second and third fingers ready to steal ball as cup comes down.

3. Ball is gripped quickly by the second and third fingers – cup is tilted forward.

4. Ball is pressed into palm.

5. With the ball safely palmed hand moves away as cup is placed down on table.

6. Ball is here seen being dropped into cup secretly.

So far, so good—but the cup's upside down now, isn't it? So it is, but that needn't trouble you. With a turn of the hand, bring it mouth down and place it on the table, all in one sweeping movement. The ball will be trapped there, to be revealed next time you lift the cup.

These are some of the basic moves in the Cups and Balls trick, but they're by no means the only moves. In one book I've just picked at random from my shelves—*Cups and Balls Magic,* by Mitchell Kanter, of Philadelphia—there are no fewer than 56 chapters, each devoted to a different move or secret associated with the trick. And Kanter only deals with *one* form of the Cups and Balls trick—the English and American style. Other books have been written to teach the Oriental style, the Miniature Cups and Balls, Thimble-rigging, the method of producing live birds or liquids from the cups— there's no end to the variations of the Cups and Balls trick.

The Oriental version of it is particularly colourful and spectacular, but because it means learning a completely new technique, it's not often practised by European or American magicians.

The Indians and the Chinese use a small wooden cup, shaped like half a sphere, and bearing a knob on the top. This is turned on a lathe and usually bears coloured grooves round its outer surface. The balls used are made of cotton, wrapped in a fine silk net. The Oriental magician will do the trick on the floor, and will finish with a climax in which he places an empty cup on your outstretched hand. When you lift the cup, you will find several balls under it!

The technique for this particular version calls for a presentation below the eye-level of the spectators, which means either that you must work on the floor, or that you must order your audience to stand up! A few European magicians have evolved a compromise and can perform a good routine on a table, but somehow it lacks the odd effect of the trick when it's performed on the floor.

The Japanese do the Cups and Balls trick, too, and they make it even more difficult, using very shallow wide cups which are more like our saucers than the usual cups used in the trick.

These are handled by the edge, with the fingertips, and I have yet to see a European attempt this version.

The nearest approach to the Japanese version is said to be the method used in Persia. Rezvani, the Persian magician, who lives in Paris, where he is a teacher of Oriental languages, performs a beautiful traditional version of the Persian system. Seated on the floor, he uses two wide-mouthed bowls and a number of woollen balls, which he calls tomatoes. The balls skip miraculously from bowl to bowl, and although magicians know how he does the trick (for he explained it fully in his book, *Rezvanie Magie*) they are quite unable to follow the moves Rezvani uses.

The notorious "Three Shell Game" has become respectable of late years, and many conjurers present it as the conjuring trick it really is, and not as the race-course swindle it has been for so long. Some magicians use walnut shells and a small "pea" made of rubber, but lately there has come on the magical market a beautiful little set of miniature cups and balls, made of polished wood or plastic. They are modelled on the Oriental cups, but the technique used is the actual method employed by swindlers in the Three Shells Game. Many improvements have been added, so that by now, most conjurers who know this trick could pretty well confound any race-course trickster by finding the pea under any shell they wish! The original Three Shell Game is heavily loaded in favour of the "operator." He can make a ball appear under any shell, or show any shell empty. You have not the slightest chance of winning when the "operator" doesn't want you to win.

Over the years, the number of tricks based on the "One in Three" puzzle of the Three Shell Game has grown surprisingly. It started, probably, with the trick wherein three matchboxes are laid down. One rattles, because it has matches in it. The others are empty. The conjurer moves the boxes round, and you are challenged to find the rattler. You'll rarely find it, except by chance, because the box that rattles isn't the one on the table. It's another box, containing a few lead shot, tied to the conjurer's wrist under his sleeve.

Then came the trick with the three little bells. The principle was exactly the same. The bell that rang was really a fourth bell, hidden in the sleeve.

Magicians are always trying to improve on these old tricks—which may not be such a good thing. The Cups and Balls, the Three Shell Game, the matchboxes, the bells, became stale and someone invented the Rattle Bars. These are three short metal bars. One of them is hollow, and contains a ball-bearing, which rattles when the bar is shaken. The other two are solid. But this time, the fourth bar, the secret bar that also rattles, isn't up the magician's sleeve. It's sometimes contained in a cigarette which he holds in the hand manipulating the bars, sometimes in a pencil.

One of the latest of the One in Three tricks is a really handsome invention—three lipstick cases, in gilt. Again, one rattles, because it apparently has a lipstick in it. The other two are silent. You may pick up the lipsticks and examine them. You may follow the routine with one finger held against the "rattler," but when you pick it up—it doesn't rattle any more!

This is a mechanical trick, using the three lipsticks and nothing else. There is no fourth lipstick concealed anywhere. There is no sleight of hand. It just works! And if you wish to know *how* it works, I suggest you buy a set, if you can find an owner willing to part with one!

Having mentioned these offshoots of the Three in One puzzle, it would be a pity to omit from this chapter the best known of all—"Find the Lady."

Almost any conjurer can perform this trick, with ordinary cards picked from your own pack, better than the race-course trickster. There's nothing difficult in 'it, and the more slowly it's presented, the more baffling it seems to become. Not long ago, David Nixon showed Find the Lady on television, using three genuine, ordinary cards. He invited viewers to write to him, telling him where they thought the "Lady" might be in the line-up of three cards when he'd finished the trick. Oddly enough, although everyone had one chance in three of guessing correctly, *less than one-third* of those who wrote got it right.

And they say the TV camera can't fool anyone with sharp eyes!

If you'd like to learn "Find the Lady," take a picture card and two pip cards. One pip card is picked up in the left hand between thumb at one end and second finger at the other end. The right hand does the work. The second pip card is placed

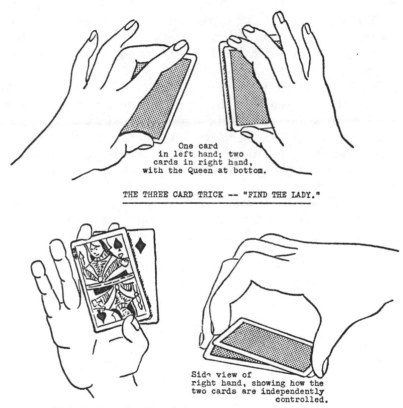

One card
in left hand; two
cards in right hand,
with the Queen at bottom.

THE THREE CARD TRICK -- "FIND THE LADY."

Side view of
right hand, showing how the
two cards are independently
controlled.

Right hand -- view from below.

between right thumb and forefinger, while the picture card goes between right thumb and *second* finger. Now, when the cards are first thrown down on the table, the right hand drops the queen, the left hand drops its card, and the right hand drops its pip card. The three cards are moved around—face-down of course—on the table. Even working the trick honestly, like this, you'll find that many people can't follow the queen in her travels. However, the first run—the honest one!—is followed by one in which the magician cheats!

Again, right hand throws down a card, followed by the left hand's card, and again one from the right hand. But this time, instead of first throwing down the queen (which is the lower of the two right-hand cards) the *upper* card is thrown down first.

The secret of the trick's success lies in making the two movements look alike, exactly and precisely alike. And so the audience cannot tell whether the queen is dropped first, or third.

You'd like to try that? You shall.

First, be sure you have the right hold for the cards. Lay a card down before you on the table. Place the thumb at the inner end and the second finger at the outer end. Pick up the card. Practise this until you can pick the card up, with either hand, without looking at it. Just the thumb tip and the finger tip do the picking up.

That's how a single card is held in the hand. Now pick up a card using the *forefinger* and the thumb. To hold a second card in the same hand, use the second finger and the thumb. You will find that by opening the first two fingers, when you have two cards held like this, the two cards will swivel out into a "V" shape. The thumb holds one end of each card, but the outer end of each card is independently controlled, the pip card by the forefinger, and the queen by the second finger. The queen is the lower card, and is the first to be dropped at this stage. But don't drop it straight down. Bring the right hand in a sweeping movement, from right to left, and allow the queen to fall as the hand passes in front of the body. Now carry the right hand back to the right, and repeat the move with the left hand, letting that card fall in the same manner. Then drop the third card from the right hand.

It's as simple as that—when the trick's done in a straightforward manner! But, oh, the cheating that can creep in!

The simplest method of cheating is for the operator to miscall the card he picks up. For example, someone points to the middle card and says: "That's the Queen!" If it *isn't* the Queen, the swindler turns it up towards himself, so that the spectator can't see the face of the card, and says: "That's right." He pays out, having apparently lost that bet. He then picks up the cards again in a very straightforward manner, and lays them out this time very slowly. He does this so slowly, in fact, as to make quite sure that the card picked up as the Queen can be followed without the least difficulty.

This time, the bets are higher. The victim is sure he's followed the "Queen" faithfully, and bets heavily. But of course, on turning the cards up, he finds that he's been had. It never *was* the Queen!

Another ruse is worked by the operator's confederate. For a moment, the swindler's attention is distracted, and he looks away from the cards. While his head is turned, the confederate winks at the audience (of which he seems to be a member) and turns up the cards swiftly, showing the Queen and bending a corner of it, to identify it. He points to the kink in the corner of the Queen, winks knowingly, and then assumes an innocent aspect as the operator turns back to the cards.

This time, you'd think, it's impossible to miss. The Queen has a bend in the corner. All we have to do is to back the card with a bent corner. And so you do, alas!

For when the cards are turned face-up, the Queen is quite straight, while *another* card has a bent corner! The operator, of course, has taken out one bend, and put another in.

Even if you *do* spot the Queen as the face-down cards are laid down, it won't be the Queen when the cards are turned over. By turning over one card with another card, the operator can exchange the two cards imperceptibly by sleight of hand. This move is known to conjurers as "The Mexican Turnover." If ever you are tempted to play "Find the Lady"—and I sincerely hope you won't be so foolish!—*stop* when the operator uses one card to turn over the card you've bet on. Stop playing—*playing!*—and walk right away.

The same goes for the Three Shell Game, too. Never, never play it under any circumstances. You *can't* win at either game unless the operator wants you to win.

But if you want to see a piece of first-class sleight of hand, watch a conjurer perform the Cups and Balls trick. And, as I said at the beginning of this chapter, if you really want to appreciate the skill called for, go and try to do the same trick yourself. Buy all the magic books that ever mentioned the Cups and Balls, study them all, and then try again. You'll still need months of practice.

Unless, of course, you care to perform the trick by means of telekinesis. In which case, I'd like to meet you. So, no doubt, would M.I.5. . . .

Chapter Three

ORACLES AND ROBOTS

> ROBOT. Term derived from the Czech word
> meaning "Work," and signifying an automaton
> in human form. It was first coined by Karel
> Capek in his play "R.U.R." (1921).

THAT'S WHAT my encyclopedia has to say about robots. Surprising, isn't it, that we've only had the word since 1921? *But we've had robots among us for thousands of years.*

From the ancient Egyptians onwards, there have been "living" images of gods and demons recorded in the annals of most of the world's religions. When the priests of Bel invited Daniel to worship their god, their king said to the Prophet: "Doth not Bel seem to thee to be a living god? Seest thou not how much he eateth and drinketh every day?"

Bel, though, was but a poor imitation of an automaton. True, the food and drink set out for him was always consumed after the doors of the temple had been locked and sealed. There was apparently no way into the temple except through the sealed doors. That's true, too.

But Daniel saw through the priests' impostures, and exposed them to the king by having ashes sifted on the floor of the temple. When the doors were unlocked, the food and drink had gone, but footprints leading from the altar to a secret door gave the whole game away.

So you can hardly call Bel either a robot or an automaton, nor could you describe the priests as very skilful magicians. Indeed, I only mention the priests of Bel (or Baal, as he is generally known) as an instance of ancient deception. Even to the disciples of their cult they can't have seemed very convincing. After all, what's so mysterious about a dish of food and a flagon of wine being emptied? They could have done

19

better than that, those priests of Bel, if only they'd thought a little more deeply.

Their predecessors of ancient Egypt certainly did better. In *their* temples, doors opened without any man touching them, images suddenly came to life and poured libations of wine and oil upon the altar fires, statues spoke and moved, mysterious voices whispered and boomed from nowhere. It must have been baffling in the extreme to the poor worshipper.

In fact, it would probably be quite baffling to any of us today, until we dismissed it all with one word—"Clockwork!"

If the ancient Egyptian, and later, the ancient Greek and Roman, had thought of that solution (yes, I know; they didn't have "clock" work then. But I'm still going to use the word), he'd have been wrong. But if he'd hinted that hydraulic power was being used, he'd have been very near the truth in most cases of oracular skulduggery. Hydraulics, pneumatics, and concealed tubing provided the means of accomplishing much of the mystery of the temples in the ancient world.

Water leaking through a tap in a hidden cistern provided the power for the movement of doors and images. As the level of the water rose, a float connected to a pivoted arm set the mechanism in motion.

What a come-down it is for that same mechanism to operate the flushing of our modern toilets!

Steam activated by the altar fires, with the water container inside the altar itself, caused the libations to be poured upon the altars. And to think that today we sit and watch our coffee percolator bubbling away on the dining room table, and never give a thought to the mysteries of the Temples of Isis!

And as for concealed tubes bringing voices to us—why, *I* have a tube that brings voices *and* pictures to my easy chair. So have you, if you own a television set.

But if you want to see a fine old example of a speaking tube in use, you should visit Davenport's Magic Shop in London, where you'll hear George Davenport shout down such a tube to a mysterious basement where the stock is kept. So it may be that the last of the speaking tubes has come to a fitting resting place. From the Delphic Oracle to Davenports. From the Nile to New·Oxford Street.

And from such deep thoughts let's move on to the more characteristic robots. By that, I mean automata in human form. Would you be surprised if I told you that you could see man-like robots at work every day in the centre of London, right out in the open air? What's more, you wouldn't have to pay a single penny to watch them at their work—useful work, it is, too, useful and decorative.

You doubt that? All right. Walk to London's Fleet Street, and stand on the pavement opposite St. Dunstan's Church. There you'll see mechanical figures striking the hours and the quarters on the great clock in the tower. You'll see a similar thing if you go to look at the clock outside Liberty's famous store in Regent Street. The clock there, incidentally, is just around the corner and not in Regent Street itself, which is perhaps a good thing. I'd hate to think that this book could be the cause of stopping the traffic in Regent Street. . . .

Clockwork robots, using "clockwork" in the literal sense, seem to have been the original forebears of the automata later associated with the conjurer's art. In Nuremberg, from the 14th century onwards, clockmakers delighted in constructing elaborate timepieces with performing figures to strike the hours and the quarters.

In the 15th century there was one particular craftsman whose name became a legend—Johann Muller, known as Regiomontanus. Some of his fabrications sound pretty legendary, too. He is said, for example, to have built an eagle which, upon the approach of the Emperor Maximilian, in June, 1470, perched upon the town gate. More than that, the knowing bird stretched out its wings, bowed, and saluted the Emperor by an inclination of the body.

Regiomontanus also delighted his friends with an iron fly he had made, which would flit from his hand, fly round the room, and return to his hand. That's hard to believe, but then, so are many of the tales of Regiomontanus's automata. At the same time, Regiomontanus's friends may have *thought* they saw something like the trick I've described. Conjurers today perform a trick in which a fly is seen perched on a small ivory paddle, held in the left hand. At the word of command, it jumps to another paddle held in the right hand.

But this fly isn't made of iron, and Regiomontanus certainly had no hand in making the one I use, which came from a magic shop and cost fifteen shillings.

A notable dabbler in the science of making automata was Charles V, Ruler of the Holy Roman Empire and King of Spain, the Netherlands, Naples, Sicily, and a great part of the New World (1500-1558). Three years before he died, Charles V abdicated and passed the remainder of his days in the monastery of Yuste, in Spain, where, historians say, "he entered with zest into the study of mechanism."

With one Torriano, an eminent artist, he built mechanical puppets which beat drums, blew trumpets, and went through the motions of drill and combat. Charles's wooden sparrows, which flew round the monastery, put the monks into a frenzy of fear. I can sympathise with them. I feel the same when I walk near those immature characters who fly tethered model aircraft in London's parks.

The wealthier citizens of pre-revolutionary Paris had an extraordinary predilection for automata. The *Memoires de l'Académie des Sciences* for 1729 report a curious toy built for Louis XIV by an artificer named Truchet. This was a complete model theatre which staged an opera in five acts, with tiny moving figures each performing separate rôles.

The famous craftsman, Camus, also constructed mechanical set-pieces for the French Royal family. One of Camus' masterpieces was a small carriage, drawn by two horses, and carrying a lady of fashion, with a coachman to drive and a footman and page hanging on behind. When placed on the floor the horses galloped along, the coachman cracked his whip, and the coach stopped. The page then descended from his perch on the rear axle, opened the door, and the lady stepped out. With a curtsey, she bowed and presented a petition to the King. She then bowed again, and entered the carriage. The page clambered up to his perch, the coachman cracked his whip, the horses galloped off, the footman ran behind . . . Phew!

But all these ingenious craftsmen were mere dilettantes. The first real master of the mechanical men was Jacques de Vaucanson, born at Grenoble on February 24th, 1709, of a noble family.

On May 3rd, 1738, there appeared this notice in the
Memoires de l'Académie des Sciences:—

The Academy, after hearing Monsieur de Vaucanson's
memoir read, containing a description of a wooden statue,
copied from Coysvoix's marble faun, which plays twelve
different airs on a German flute with a precision deserving of
public attention, was of opinion that this machine was
extremely ingenious; that the inventor had employed novel
and simple means, both to give the fingers the necessary
motion and to modify the wind entering the flute, by augment-
ing or diminishing its velocity, according to the various tones;
by varying the arrangement of the lips, and setting a valve in
motion to perform the functions of the tongue; lastly, by
artificially imitating all that a man is obliged to do; and that,
in addition, Monsieur de Vaucanson's memoir possessed all
the clearness and perception such matter is capable of, proving
the intelligence of the author, and his great knowledge of the
different branches of mechanism. In confirmation of which I
have signed the present certificate.

Fontenelle,
Perpetual Secretary, Royal Academy of Sciences.
Paris, May 3rd, 1738.

Vaucanson exhibited three automata in Paris that year—the
flute player, a tambourine player, and an artificial duck. More
than a hundred years later, his robot musicians inspired John
Nevil Maskelyne to produce similar automata.

Vaucanson himself published explanations of his life-size
automata, and that, no doubt, set the magicians of a later day
working on illusions using mechanical figures.

One of the first illusions using an automaton was the famous
chess-playing figure built by Baron Wolfgang von Kempelen,
which baffled the crowned heads of the world. Von
Kempelen's Chess Player is still the subject for argument among
magicians. Those who don't know how it worked will argue
as to its mechanical principles. Those who do know how it
worked will debate its whereabouts today.

There's quite a story attached to the Chess Player. It was
built by von Kempelen in 1769, in the form of an Oriental

pasha, seated on a bench behind a large table. On the table
was a chess-board and chessmen. The table had a large cup-
board beneath it, containing the mechanism which operated
the Chess Player, and by opening various doors and drawers,
the whole of the interior could be—and was—shown to the
audience.

VON KEMPELEN'S
AUTOMATON
CHESS PLAYER

(But it wasn't
an automaton!)

The left hand
(holding the pipe) was
a dummy. When the operator
removed the pipe, he also took away
the hand, and the hidden assistant thrust
his own hand down the figure's sleeve.

The figure of the Chess Player was much smaller than life-
size, and was by no means big enough to contain a man,
although the theory of a concealed assistant was invariably
advanced as an explanation of the mystery by those who had
not seen the illusion worked. But when the mechanism was
thrown open to public view, and the audience had the chance
of examining the inside of the cupboards, it was conceded that
no assistant could possibly find space to hide himself inside the
"works."

It was many years before the secret of its working leaked out, and in that time the Chess Player not only played games of chess with most of the notabilities of Europe, but won those games. Baron von Kempelen died on March 26th, 1804, and his son sold the Chess Player to a Bavarian named J. N. Maelzel. Although Maelzel was a musician and inventor in his own right (he invented the metronome), he devoted himself to a new career as showman, and travelled all over the world with the Chess Player, taking on all challengers at the game. And, incidentally, he made for himself a respectable little fortune from his mystery.

It was an impressive show that he gave. When the audience were seated, a pair of crimson velvet curtains would be drawn open slowly, and Maelzel would make his entrance. He would then introduce the automaton.

This is how Henry Ridgely Evans, the great historian of magic, described the scene:—

Behind the box or table, which was two feet and a half high, three feet and a half long, and two feet wide, was seated cross-legged the figure of a Turk. The chair on which the figure was affixed was permanently attached to the box. At the top of the box was a chess-board. The figure had its eyes fixed intently upon this board, its right hand and arm being extended towards the board, its left, which was somewhat raised, holding a long pipe.

Four doors, two in front and two in the rear of the box, were opened, and a lighted candle was thrust into the cavities. Nothing was to be seen except cogwheels, levers, and intricate machinery. A long drawer, which contained the chessmen and a cushion, was pulled out. Two doors in the Turk's body were thrown open, and the candle was held inside, to satisfy the spectators that nothing but machinery was contained therein.

Maelzel wound up the machinery with a large key, took away the pipe, and placed the cushion under the arm of the figure. Curious to relate, the automaton played with its left hand. In von Kempelen's day, the person selected to play with the figure sat at the same chess-board with it, but Maelzel altered this. A rope separated the machine from the audience, and the player sat at a small table, provided with a chess-board, some ten or twelve feet away from the Turk.

The automaton invariably chose the white chessmen and made the first move, its fingers opening as the hand was extended towards the board, and the piece picked up and removed to its proper square.

When his antagonist had made his move, the automaton paused and appeared to study the game before proceeding further. It nodded its head to indicate check to the King. If a false move was made by its opponent, it rapped on the table, and replaced the piece, claiming the move for itself. Maelzel, acting for the human player, repeated his move on the chess-board of the Turk, and when the latter moved, made the corresponding move on the board of the challenger. The whirring of machinery was heard during the progress of the game. . . .

Marvellous, the sight must have been! Not that the Turk won *every* game, but there was an explanation for those occasions on which he lost. It was a reasonable, logical explanation, but the public never heard it.

In fact, the only times when the Turk lost a game were those when the man inside wasn't quite sober!

Yes, there was a man inside the automaton. His name was Wilhelm Schlumberger, and he was a native of Alsace, and an expert chess player and linguist. The whirring of machinery which accompanied the game was useful to disguise his hiccups and muttered exclamations when he'd been at the bottle, as well as to cover the sound of his movements from one part of the box to another when the doors were flung open.

Although there wasn't room inside either the box or the figure of the Turk for a man to hide when *all* the doors were opened at once, there was sufficient space when the doors were opened one or two at a time. These doors would then be closed, and, to the accompaniment of the sound of machinery in action, Schlumberger would shift his position to that part of the box which had just been shown empty. Then more doors would be opened to show his previous hiding place, now empty.

Edgar Allen Poe was probably the first layman to break down Maelzel's mystery. Poe noticed that Schlumberger had no ostensible occupation other than packing and unpacking the automaton. He also noticed that Schlumberger, although frequently visible before and after the exhibitions, was never seen while the chess games were being played. When Schlumberger was taken ill, in Richmond, Virginia, the exhibitions were called off.

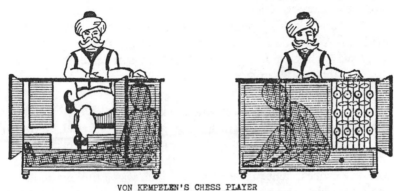

VON KEMPELEN'S CHESS PLAYER
(Above) How the man in the box hid himself when the doors were open.

(Below) He takes up his position ready for play when the doors are closed.

Schlumberger died of yellow fever in Cuba, and Maelzel himself died on the voyage home, in 1838. The Chess Player was sold by auction in Philadelphia, and was bought by Dr. J. K. Mitchell, who reconstructed it and showed it for the entertainment of his friends. Later, it was deposited in a museum, where it remained until the building was burnt down in 1854. Some say the automaton was destroyed in the fire. Some say it was saved.

One man today might be able to settle this question once and for all. He is Guy Bert, a famous Parisian magician, in whose workrooms reposes the figure of a little Turk, seated at a table with a chess-board in front of him. . . .

And now let's travel back from 20th century Paris to the London of 1875. The whole town's talking about Mr. Maskelyne's latest mystery. At the Egyptian Hall, where Maskelyne and Cooke stage their marvellous magic shows, there's a new attraction—Psycho.

Psycho is a small Oriental figure, seated cross-legged on a box, which is supported by a large cylinder of clear glass. Psycho not only plays chess, draughts and whist, but can calculate any sum up to a total of 99 million.

How is it possible?

That's the question Londoners asked themselves when they flocked to see Psycho perform. For although Maelzel, and von Kempelen before him, may have had the assistance of a concealed man in their "automaton," there was positively no room for any concealment inside Psycho, which was a tiny figure about half life size. And to make confusion thrice confounded, there was no apparent means of connection with the figure when it was perched on its glass column. No tubes or wires could be thrust through the floorboards to connect up with Psycho's works, or they'd have been seen through the glass.

Psycho had works, of course, and no secret was made of the fact. But even so, how could the works be set to deal with an unpredictable problem such as a game of chess played against a member of the audience?

Maskelyne and Cooke may themselves have revealed the secret that same year, when they applied for a patent for a method of controlling the speed of clockwork mechanism by compressed air or gas stored in the pedestal of an automaton. In their specifications, this air or gas when compressed acted upon a piston in a cylinder, and also upon a rotating fan when a valve was opened by "an electrical or other connection worked by the foot of the performer or an assistant."

The inventors *may* have given the secret away in their application for a patent. But it's far more likely that they were laughing up their sleeves when they linked their application to an automaton. Compressed air *could* have worked the mechanism, but it would be going about the job the hard way.

There are conjuring tricks being performed today which use a rare principle—moving transparent glass inside a stationary transparent glass container. The moving glass cannot be seen to move, as it is transparent. And the outer casing can neither be seen nor felt to move—because it doesn't move.

This principle could have actuated Psycho. Think it out. You could get at least eight positive movements by means of a rotating glass cylinder moving inside a stationary glass tube: (1) clockwise rotation, (2) anti-clockwise rotation, (3) vertical movement upwards, (4) vertical movement downwards, (5) clockwise rotation while moving upwards, (6) clockwise rotation while moving downwards, (7) anti-clockwise rotation while moving upwards, (8) anti-clockwise rotation while moving downwards.

Add to these, graduations of each movement, whereby a cog could be moved tooth by tooth, each step giving a different result, and you have an almost infinite series of movements and results.

If you care to reason the thing out still further, you can see Psycho for yourself. The little Hindu today sits, thoughtful and melancholy, in the London Museum, now housed in Kensington Palace.

Psycho was not the invention of Maskelyne and Cooke, but was created originally by a Lincolnshire farmer, Mr. John Clarke. Maskelyne was so impressed with the figure when he saw it that he built a large workshop to develop the farmer's invention, and it was there that he built the finished version of Psycho.

Besides being able to play chess, draughts, and whist, Psycho could smoke a cigarette, perform a few conjuring tricks, and spell. He could also give the Masonic grip, though I doubt whether he was ever taught to be cautious about this.

Psycho was a true automaton only insofar as he *contained* no hidden assistant. The concealed assistant came, I am sure, from below the stage. The mechanism inside Psycho was more essential than the maze of cog-wheels and levers inside the Chess Player. Psycho's works were responsible, I believe, for converting the eight movements of the glass cylinder into the necessary motions associated with the feats performed by the figure.

Two years after Psycho made his first bow, Maskelyne introduced another automaton to London—Zoe, the drawing figure. Zoe was, in the words of Jasper Maskelyne, "a charming little mechanical lady, who could sketch the profile of any celebrity chosen by the audience, and sketch it with the hand of a master of the pencil. Zoe sat on a slender mahogany pedestal in the centre of the stage, and held a pencil. A sheet of paper on a drawing board was suspended in front of her. Before each performance, a committee of inspection from the audience was invited to come and examine the little lady, and discover, if possible, the secret of her powers."

Zoe had a distinguished ancestor, created a century earlier by Henri-Louis Jacquet-Droz, a Swiss mechanician from Neuchatel. The works of Jacquet-Droz remain famous until this day, and the Swiss clockwork singing birds prized as parlour ornaments are built upon the principles he and his father, Pierre Jacquet-Droz, perfected.

The Jacquet-Droz writing figure was a true automaton, as apart from a piece of mechanism needing the use of concealed helpers. It was modelled like a young boy, seated at a table with a pen in his hand. When the clockwork was set in motion, he would look at the sheet of paper before him, move his hand to the ink-pot, and dip in the pen. He would then shake off any excess of ink from the pen, and start to write.

The operation involved a notched disc, bearing a notch for each letter and punctuation sign, in which a pawl was engaged. Each letter was formed by the rotation of a cam, specially shaped for each sign the figure was to make. Levers and cardan joints in the arm were set in motion by a system of chain-operated sprocket wheels.

Jacquet-Droz also made a drawing figure, the mechanism of which was even more elaborate.

It might be thought that Maskelyne's Zoe would have put Psycho out of business, but alas! she proved nowhere near as popular as the meditative little Hindu.

Zoe was separated from the floor of the stage by a sheet of glass, which to a conjurer would prove an even more baffling obstacle to the operation of the figure than had the glass cylinder of Psycho. But Maskelyne found no difficulty in communicating mechanical impulses through glass. In those days, the theory and practice of electro-magnetism wasn't in wide use, and it seems to me that therein lay the secret of Zoe. With an adequate train of gears inside the figure, a helper beneath the stage would only need to move an electro-magnet along the lines of the drawing to be copied, to have the hand of the figure follow the same lines.

Maskelyne added two more inmates to his menagerie of automata in 1878—Fanfare and Labial. These were little figures of men who played the cornet and the euphonium respectively. Their lip movements and their fingering were said by A. J. Phasey, a noted wind instrument player of the day, to be perfect. Their tone and execution, too, were of high standard.

The difficulty here, no doubt, would be to make the mechanical figures and their lip and finger movements synchronise exactly with the sound produced by a back-stage player of each instrument. For that is probably how the *sound* was produced— by instrumentalists playing behind a semi-transparent curtain immediately behind the figures, so as to produce the sound from approximately the right direction.

Today, with the miracles of radio and television in every home, the novelty of automata is outdated. Not many years ago, as time goes, this present writer as a child loved nothing better than to drop a penny into one of those mechanical tableaux to be found at the end of every seaside pier. For a penny, ghosts would rise shuddering from behind some inoffensive citizen's bed, while skeletons popped jerkily out from behind the pictures, and horned red demons jiggled about in the background.

What a thrill, compared with today's automatic penn-orths! Who could muster any enthusiasm for a ball that rolls between chromium-plated obstacles, clocking up a score of several million though it may?

But automata still remain with us. Mainly, today, they are the costly prizes of collectors such as my friend Roland Winder, a Leeds engineer, whose speciality is the collection of miniature automata. Mr. Winder's show-pieces are small masterpieces of craftsmanship such as a gold snuffbox which produces a tiny feathered bird when a projection is pressed. Up pops the bird, turning its head and flapping its wings, as it sings a short song. Then, on the last note, it vanishes and the snuffbox is silent.

One of the rarities in this line—though a silent performer—is a small figure of a magician who performs the Cups and Balls trick on a table. He lifts one cup and shows a ball there. He replaces the cup, lifts it again, and the ball is gone, to appear under another cup. This little robot—if you can find one in perfect working order—is worth a small fortune.

It's good to know that he's appreciated by someone these days —even if he doesn't mystify us any longer.

Chapter Four

IT'S ALL DONE WITH MIRRORS!

THE GHOSTS walked in Regent Street, London, in 1863. Not once, but for many nights in succession, and thousands of people saw them.

They saw a medieval student, studying an ancient black-letter folio by the light of a flickering lamp. As the clocks struck the hour of midnight, they saw the student assailed by phantoms. A skeleton, robed in a shroud, arose screaming through the floor of the student's room. The crowds saw the young man—less daunted than the spectators!—draw a naked sword and pursue the ghost through a series of wild gyrations. The blade passed again and again through the ghost, which mocked the student and defied his sword until the young man fell in a swoon to the floor. Then—a flash of bright light, and the ghost was gone.

That was it. And plenty, too.

And as the crowds left the Polytechnic Institute, where the ghost show was staged, they were agog with theories. There were even many who were sure they'd seen genuine occultism in practice. Others, less gullible, had ingenious theories very far from the truth. A few—the less agile minds, oddly enough—dismissed it all as today's dimmer wits dismiss some modern magic: "It's all done with mirrors, of course!"

They were right. It *was* all done with mirrors.

But even though the truth wasn't slow to leak out, the crowds still flocked to pay their shillings and half-crowns to see Professor John Henry Pepper's ghosts.

Pepper's Ghost. Born 1863, and still going strong. Mind you, in the ninety-odd years since he first walked the boards in Regent Street, Pepper's Ghost has changed his name—and his sex—many times. He and his related offspring may be known as The Phantom of the Blue Room, as The Headless Girl, as The Princess of Bakhten, as The Sphinx, as Les Phantomes du

33

Cabaret du Néant. By their names you will never know them. But despite their aliases, they remain—Pepper's Ghost.

We know him, whatever he may call himself. But do *you*?

Have you ever carried a lighted candle to a dark window, and looked out? What have you seen? Who is that other figure, surprisingly like yourself, carrying a lighted candle on the other side of the glass?

That is Pepper's Ghost.

John Henry Pepper, Professor of Chemistry at the Polytechnic, and Henry Dircks, civil engineer, although they weren't the first to see the ghost in the glass, were the first to patent him. It was in 1863 that they took out letters patent to cover their discovery, and within weeks they were drawing full houses to the Polytechnic's lecture hall, where the ghost gibbered every night.

If you like to reproduce Pepper's Ghost in your own parlour you can, but the cost these days will be pretty steep. You'll need a sheet of plate-glass the width of the room and half as high again as the ceiling; you'll need an articulated skeleton; and you'll need a sizeable hole in the floor. Those were the items Pepper provided for his audiences.

His stage was a small one, of course, but even so, that sheet of glass had to fill it. It was laid on the tilt, from a line half-way up the stage at its lower edge, to the inner side of the proscenium arch at the upper edge. Behind it the "living" actors played their part. In front of it yawned a cavity eight feet deep and eight feet wide, running the full width of the stage. And down in that hole dwelt the ghost.

The audience never saw the hole, of course, because they were placed below the level of the edge of the stage. All they saw was the actor behind the glass, and the reflected image of the ghost in the underground chamber. When a light was shone on the ghost, he was reflected in the sheet of glass. When the light went out, the ghost went out, too. It was as simple as that. But it brought in a pretty penny to the Poly and to Pepper.

The skeleton, of course, couldn't move about by itself, and so a man carried it, horizontal, and manipulated its bones. The audience never saw this character, for the simple reason that he was dressed from top to toe in black velvet. The cavity was painted black inside, so that he merged into the background, while the white skeleton stood out plainly as a reflection in the tilted glass.

Today's camera trickery on television is a direct descendant of Pepper's Ghost. When you see David Nixon hobnobbing with tiny dwarf figures on the arm of his chair, you may think of Pepper, and the Polytechnic of 1863. Nixon can't see the figures which appear on your screen (though he might take a peep at

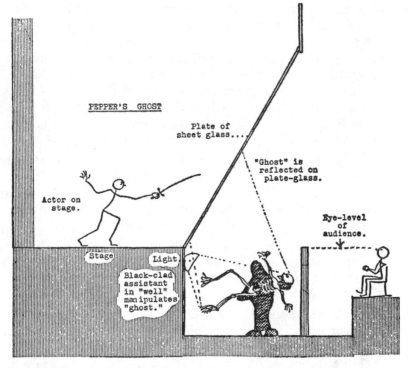

PEPPER'S GHOST

Plate of sheet glass...

"Ghost" is reflected on plate-glass.

Actor on stage.

Eye-level of audience.

Stage   Light

Black-clad assistant in "well" manipulates "ghost."

the monitor set to make sure all's well) and neither could the actor at the Poly see *his* ghost. But all was worked out to a fraction of a second and to a fraction of an inch. Marks on the stage guided the actor through his ghastly sword combat, so that although the ghost was invisible to him, he knew where it *ought* to be. And similar marks in the pit below the plate of glass showed the black-clad ghost-walker where to stand.

A dim light behind the glass ensured that the image of the ghost was reflected boldly, brightly-lit as it was itself.

Simple—but *so* convincing.

Pepper's Ghost had a long and distinguished line of ancestors, stretching away back to ancient Egypt, to Chaldea, to Babylon. In the lost continents of Atlantis and Mu, according to the legends, the spirits of the gods appeared to men.

Back in those distant days, though, it was the silvered mirror that was responsible. Pepper's sheet of plain glass was the main Victorian stem of the ghost's pedigree. The ancients made great play with concave mirror projections, thus contriving to show varying sizes of ghosts. Using a darkened wall of the temple, or the smoke from the altar fires as their screen, they could show you Osiris or Adonis, Esculapius or Hecate, Ahriman or Ashteroth. The priests and their acolytes must have found it hard not to laugh during these solemn manifestations, not only because of the devout manner in which the worshippers accepted their illusions, but because the unseen actor representing the god *had to be upside down, in order to be reflected right way up!*

They were clever enough to discover and make use of the properties of a hollowed-out mirror. You'd think they'd have had the sense to devise a means whereby they could project an image the right way up. But, apparently, no. Perhaps that's why, even today, wizardry is a topsy-turvy business.

For hundreds of years the believers marvelled at the dim, flickering images of "the gods" projected in the smoke of the temple fires and on the walls of the shrines. And then, for a like time, everybody seemed to forget all about them.

In the Middle Ages they popped up again, but this time they were for the select few who sought the thrills of occultism and Black Magic. That slightly raffish sculptor, Benvenuto Cellini, went out of his way to be terrified by the Black Magicians and their mirror projections.

In his autobiography you may read that, in conversation with a Sicilian priest, he said : "Throughout my life I have had the most intense desire to see or learn something of this (the Black Magic) art." If that wasn't sticking his neck out, I don't know what was. Anyway, the priest replied : "A stout soul and a steadfast must the man have who sets himself to such an enterprise." Which is what the modern sideshow men call "the come-on."

And Cellini came on, all right.

He wrote: "I answered that of strength and of steadfastness of soul I should have enough and to spare, provided I found the opportunity. Then the priest said: 'If you have the heart to dare it, I will amply satisfy your curiosity.' "

And he did. Off they went to the Colosseum, a dismal place by night if ever there was one. There, "the priest, having arrayed himself in necromancer's robes, began to describe circles on the earth with the finest ceremonies that can be imagined. I must say that he had made us bring precious perfumes and fire, and also drugs of fetid odour.

"When the preliminaries were completed, he made the entrance into the circle; and, taking us by the hand, introduced us one by one inside of it. Then he assigned our several functions; to the necromancer, his comrade, he gave the pentacle to hold; the other two of us had to look after the fire and the perfumes; and then he began his incantations. This lasted more than an hour and a half, when several legions appeared, and the Colosseum was all full of devils . . ."

They had it all their own way, those necromancers. Just as the modern producer of ghosts on the stage is safely separated from his audience by a row of footlights and the orchestra pit, so those old boys treating Benvenuto Cellini to a hair-raising night out had him where they wanted him—inside a circle, with firm instructions not to overstep the line.

If he *had* taken a good look round outside the magic circle, he'd have found one or two confederates manipulating the mirrors that threw reflections on to the smoke of the fires—which Cellini himself had to tend.

Although the spirits of the Colosseum didn't grant Cellini's wish (he wanted to be reunited with his Sicilian girl friend Angelica), he was avid for more, and went back later to the Colosseum with the sorcerer and his apprentices.

Again the business with the magic circle. Again the paraphernalia of the fires, the incense and the fetid stinks. And the necromancer "began to utter those awful invocations, calling by name on multitudes of demons who are captains of their legion . . . insomuch that in a short time the whole Colosseum was full of a hundred-fold as many as had appeared upon the first occasion . . ."

As the smoke died away, so did the hobgoblins and demons. What's more, the sorcerer, playing a double bluff, assured the trembling watchers that all they had seen was but smoke and shadows.

Sir David Brewster, canny investigator of natural magic, wrote in the early 19th century that if a magic lantern hadn't been used to hoodwink Cellini (and the magic lantern wasn't invented by Kircher until a century after Cellini had trembled in the Colosseum), then concave mirrors *were*.

"A fire is lighted, and perfumes and incense are burnt," he explains, "in order to create a ground for the images, and the beholders are rigidly confined within the pale of the magic circle. The concave mirror and the objects presented to it having been so placed that the persons within the circle could not see the aerial image of the objects by the rays directly reflected from the mirror, the work of deception was ready to begin. . . . The moment the perfumes were thrown upon the fire to produce smoke, the first wreath of smoke that rose through the place of one or more of the images would reflect them to the eyes of the spectators, and they would again disappear if the wreath was not followed by another. More and more images would be rendered visible as new wreaths of smoke arose, and the whole group would appear at once when the smoke was uniformly diffused over the place occupied by the images."

It's strange to think that, with all this expert knowledge of the properties of concave lenses and mirrors, nobody side-tracked his mind to the problem of making *moving* pictures. But that's the way it was. Nevertheless, one form or another of the magic lantern made lots of money for one after another of the exhibitors. One adventurer who turned it to profitable use was a Belgian optician, with the improbable name of Etienne Gaspard Robertson.

This Belgian Scot had, among other curious ideas, the plan for destroying a British fleet by focusing giant burning glasses on the ships. The French Revolution brought opportunity to Etienne Gaspard Robertson. Something of a conjurer and illusionist, he built himself a ghost-making machine with which he raised a remarkable number of spirits—both metaphorical and phenomenal. Did your aristocratic parent lose his head under the blade of the guillotine? Nothing easier than to see him again if you attended Robertson's seances! Did you wish to exchange a word with the unfortunate Citizen Marat? Pay your money, and there he was! Would you like a peep at Citizeness Corday in boudoir attire? A few sous more, and there she appeared.

Robertson wasn't content with just dimming the lights and throwing his pictures on to a screen. No. He did the thing properly, with all due respect to the methods so highly commended by the impressionable Cellini. Into a brazier containing lighted coals, he would throw two glasses of blood, a bottle of vitriol, a few drops of aqua fortis, and an old newspaper. Which provided him with all the smoke he needed whereon to project his pictures from the magic lantern poking through a little hole in the wall.

He *must* have had some Scottish blood in his veins, this Etienne Gaspard, not only because of his strictly non-Flemish surname, but on account of the clever publicity he planned.

So sensational were his first ghost-raising efforts, that the police banned further demonstrations. What could be better for the prestige of a ghost-raiser? The result was, of course, that when the ban was lifted, Robertson worked all the hours there were to admit audience after audience—and to take franc after franc from their willing fingers.

Looking back on those lively times, the leap from the 1790s to the 1860s doesn't seem a very long one. At any rate, though, it was long enough for the public to have forgotten, apparently, about Robertson's ghost shows.

When Pepper and Dirck started to draw the crowds to the Polytechnic, other magicians at once saw the immense value of a ghost show. But, due to the shrewdness of Pepper and Dirck in patenting the illusion, they had to buy it or hire it before they could show it. And buy it and hire it they did. Within a week or so, Pepper's Ghost was appearing all over the place, from the London Pavilion and the Canterbury Music Hall, to the Imperial Châtelet Theatre in Paris.

But it wasn't long before magicians found loopholes in the patent laws big enough for a ghost to get through—Pepper's Ghost. And, of course, there were many who claimed to have thought of it all long before Pepper and Dirck. Sylvester, "The Fakir of Oolu," said he'd invented the illusion. Robin, the French illusionist, said a loud French "Pooh!" and added the airy statement that he'd first thought of the transparent mirror principle nearly twenty years earlier.

And today I know two magicians who gravely swear that they invented the mirror illusion—separately and distinctly. They may have done for all I know. Both of them look old enough to have invented the Pyramids.

Pepper was an ingenious chap, and not one to be thwarted easily. Although pirate prestidigitators were showing versions of Pepper's Ghosts, he soon baffled them even more than they baffled their audiences. Together with a Mr. Walker, he produced another great mirror illusion which *really* had the audiences—and the other magicians—guessing. This was performed *without* a pit to hide his "ghosts." He called it "Metempsychosis," and showed that by its aid a man could be changed slowly but perceptibly to a woman, a marble statue could become endowed with life, or a suit of armour could caper about the stage almost as soon as it was assembled and shown empty.

He did this by the simple method of having his mirror half-silvered. The mirror slid vertically in grooves, so that when the clear part of the glass was before the audience they could see through it. Then, as the mirror moved, the silvered part came into view and reflected an object, hidden from the audience, which took the place of the object previously seen through the clear glass. The mirror wasn't simply a plate of glass half of which was silvered, with the other half clear. It started at one edge as clear glass, and after a foot or so the silvering was faintly applied. Then came heavier silvering, and at last a solid coating of silvering. Some of the mirrors used in later adaptations of this principle were silvered in lines, starting with thin, fine lines, and then progressing through gradually heavier lines to a solid mass of silvering.

Pepper and Walker again patented their invention, which was at once taken up by the magical fraternity. Harry Kellar, American illusionist, made great use of it in his famous "Blue

Room" illusion, which ran for many years as one of the high-lights of his show.

There are many plots used for the Blue Room. In one, the curtain rises to show the Blue Room at the back of the stage, with a suit of armour in one corner. A servant takes the armour apart to clean it, and then turns away. Almost at once, the armour becomes alive, and a mailed fist deals the servant a blow. There is a comical struggle, during which the master of the house arrives. The servant, terrified by his adventure, tells the master about it all, whereupon the owner of the armour dismantles it at once, to show that there is nobody concealed in it.

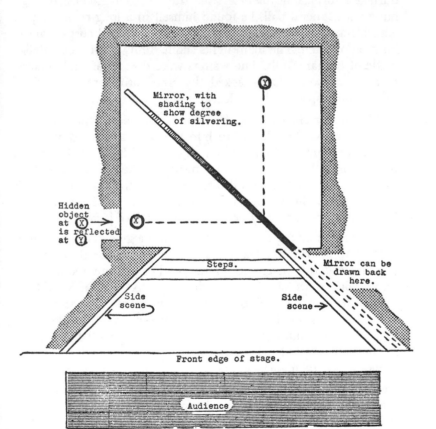

THE BLUE ROOM ILLUSION.

The illusion is brought about by the sliding mirror, which obscures the genuine suit of armour by degrees, reflecting, in exactly the same spot, a similar suit of armour with a man inside it. After the comic byplay, the mirror is withdrawn again, leaving the original armour showing.

In Paris, the illusion became famous as the Cabaret du Néant, or Tavern of the Annihilation, off the Rue Champollion in Montmartre. The original presentation was heavily melo-dramatic.

The patron entered through grim, black doors, over which burned a brimstone flame. After traversing a gloomy passage hung with funeral palls he found himself in a long room draped with black. Coffins served for tables, with a lighted corpse candle burning on each. The main lights shone dimly from a chandelier made of human skulls. The waiters were dressed as undertakers' men, and were hand-picked by the proprietor for their cadaverous aspect and sepulchral tones.

The thirsty client would be assailed by one of these *croque-morts,* who would sidle up to him much as a friendly vampire might approach a plump victim, and would be invited to name his poison. "We have on tap distilled grave worms, deadly microbes, the bacteria of all diseases under the sun," the waiter would cajole. But whatever the client called for, he always got beer—and not very good beer, or very much of it, at that.

After this libation to Charon, he would be guided down a flight of creaking stairs through a creaking door (so you see, the television producers *didn't* invent it!) into another sombre room, again hung with palls and funeral drapings. A curtain would be opened to reveal a stage set as a mouldy crypt, with an upright coffin standing in the middle. A volunteer would be placed in the coffin, a winding sheet would be placed round him, and a strong light would be shone on him.

Then, gradually, he would change to a skeleton. The flesh would seem to peel from his face. His eyes would slowly fade into black sockets, the nose would be replaced by a cavity. A church bell would be tolled, and two pseudo monks would chant: "He dies! He wastes away! Dust to dust! The eternal worm awaits you all!" The organ would play a miserable dirge, the bell would toll, and after a moment, even the skeleton would fade out, leaving a heap of shrouds in its place.

Then the unfortunate volunteer would slowly begin to re-appear. The music would fade, the bell recede into the distance, the chanting die down. And before you could say "Alas! Poor volunteer; I knew him well!" the fellow would be back in the upright coffin, grinning sheepishly.

The performance ended by the mock monks passing round the crowd to take up a collection in a human skull.

Ah well, anything for a laugh.

Nowadays, of course, the Blue Room practitioners in Paris have added a suggestion (and suggestion is the right word) of levity to the illusion. The volunteer sits himself on a couch, instead of standing in a coffin. And the things that apparently happen to him! But that's another story altogether.

However, performed as a crypt concerto or as a suggestive scena as may be; it's still the Blue Room. Which means to say that it's still Pepper's Ghost, but a little modified, a little sophisticated, and a little Europeanised. The mirror is still there, partly silvered. And so are the unseen (by the audience) accoutrements of skeleton or glamour girl.

Incidentally, and solely in the cause of science, I have to report that customers who flip chewing gum, lead shot, or 50-franc-pieces at the pane of glass are not welcomed a second time by the Blue Room boys of Paris. One famous Montmartre resort showing a Blue Room illusion during the latter part of the last war rather spoiled the effect by using a mirror with a four-foot crack running from the edge. A G.I. with a catapult had left his mark upon the invisible sheet of glass. When I asked the proprietor why he did not have a new mirror, he seemed rather angry, and pointed out that this commodity—when it could be bought—used to cost him £160 a time. And as long as there was a G.I. left in Paris he intended to use the cracked mirror, even if there were a million cracks in it. And if they shattered it beyond repair, he added with philosophy, then he'd just have to do without it—and show the girls without the intervening mirror.

One of the most dramatic and brilliant illusions ever devised —The Princess of Bakhten—was derived from the Blue Room effect. Conceived by Stuart Luciene, it first appeared in the pages of that storehouse of magical lore, *The Magic Wand* quarterly. The plot of The Princess of Bakhten comes direct from ancient Egypt, and is contained in a papyrus written in the year 1333 B.C. and now stored in the British Museum.

The papyrus tells the story of the Princess of Bakhten, chief wife of the Pharaoh Rameses II, who was bewitched by Set, the Evil One. The wise men of the Pharaoh's court claimed that a cure could be effected if the Princess was sent to consort with the spirits of the underworld for a time. They disguised her as a mummified body, complete with all its wrappings, and placed her in a sarcophagus in the tomb. As they watched, the Pharaoh and his courtiers saw her Ka, or soul, leave her body and go its way. When the wrappings were opened, the Princess had vanished, and the sarcophagus was empty.

The illusion involved more than a single principle. Besides using the Blue Room method of substituting a mirror image for the living person, Luciene introduced a substitution of object *behind* the mirror, having the living, wrapped girl exchanged for a framework covered in wrappings.

He also reverted to the original Pepper's Ghost idea of having an unsilvered mirror, which he controlled by varying the lighting before and behind it, by turn.

The girl would be introduced to the stage, and would stand on a low turntable. The illusionist brings forward the wrappings and the girl stands on one end of the cloth. Then, as the low table is turned, the wrappings are moulded to her, until she is completely swathed in the long linen coils. The magician then lifts her up, and carries her into the "tomb," where she is placed in a mummy case. This case stands behind the transparent pane of glass, and at this moment the lighting in the rear section of the cabinet is full on.

Up to now there has been no exchange of anything, and no substitution. The "mummy" the audience see is the girl in her wrappings.

When the illusionist reaches that part of the story which tells about the girl's soul leaving her body, he points to the sarco-phagus, and the audience see a shadowy image of the girl apparently leaving the mummy's wrappings and fading away. The magician then enters the "tomb" and lifts out the enwrapped mummy. The shape of the girl's body can be clearly seen through the wrappings, but as the magician takes off the wrappings, they are seen to be empty. The girl has completely vanished.

At no time, the spectators are sure, has the wrapped girl been out of their sight. And yet—she must have been hidden for a moment. When?

THE PRINCESS OF BAKHTEN.

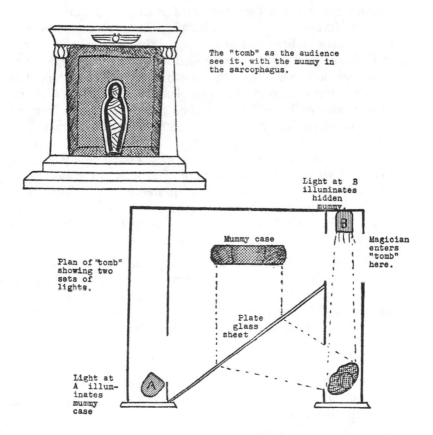

The "tomb" as the audience see it, with the mummy in the sarcophagus.

Light at B illuminates hidden mummy.

Magician enters "tomb" here.

Mummy case

Plan of "tomb" showing two sets of lights.

Plate glass sheet

Light at A illuminates mummy case

The lighting of the tomb provides the method of concealing the wrapped girl long enough to effect a substitution of the light framework wrapped with linen. It is this framework which is unwrapped at the end of the trick, and which is found empty.

There are two sets of lighting controls for the tomb. One controls the lights *behind* the diagonal pane of clear glass, and the other controls those *in front* of it. When the girl is brightly lit and the front lights are dimmed, the girl is seen clearly through the glass. When the lights illuminating her are dimmed and the front lights are developed, she fades out, and the audience see the reflection of another "mummy" which is hidden in the side walls of the tomb.

It is at this moment that the girl is carried away from the sarcophagus, and quickly unwrapped. A duplicate mummy—the wrapped framework—is put in her place in the sarcophagus, and the girl takes up her stand *at the side* of the mummy in the tomb wall. Again the lighting is controlled so that the front lights dim while the back lights brighten. This brings the real sarcophagus and its dummy mummy—!—into clear view, while the mummy in the tomb wall is obliterated. The girl then steps in front of the mummy in the wall, and the lights are changed again. This time, though, there is "half-and-half" lighting, so that both the rear and front compartments can be seen. One mummy overlaps the other, from the audience's point of view, and the girl is seen in a shadowy form in front of the mummy case. A little more manipulation of the lighting controls, and the rear compartment is lit brightly, while the front compartment—and the hidden mummy with the girl in front—is dimmed out.

The Princess of Bakhten has a complicated lighting plot, but a simple, direct effect. It is all over in a few minutes, and not for a second, the audience believe, has the wrapped girl been out of their view. They've been watching one "mummy" all the time, they think. But the fact is, they've been watching *three* mummies, one after the other!

The first is the wrapped girl; then comes the hidden mummy's reflection, followed by the mummy exchanged for the girl. It is this last object which is finally brought out by the magician and unwrapped, to be found empty.

The ingenuity of The Princess of Bakhten comes home to you when you consider the different methods used for bringing about the climax of the illusion. Transparent mirror, controlled lighting, three substitutions, and the skeleton framework.

Could *you* work out such a brilliant illusion? If you could, then I suggest you send your ideas to one or other of the few magicians performing such work today. Mind you, the odds are that you'll be "inventing" something that's been used already for many years! A new *principle* in magic is a very rare novelty. But a new *effect*—that's a different thing altogether!

Not all mirror illusions are true descendants of the Pepper's Ghost principle, which uses a transparent or semi-transparent mirror. The simpler ones—including many small tricks—use a plain mirror, either to show the reflection of a duplicate article, or, more usually, to hide an article.

Half-brother to Pepper's Ghost was The Sphinx, fathered by Thomas Tobin, also of London's Polytechnic. Tobin is forgotten now, and most magicians will tell you solemnly that The Sphinx illusion was invented by one Colonel Stodare. But Stodare's only share in making The Sphinx famous was in exhibiting it— and earning himself an international reputation on the strength of it.

Stodare was no colonel, but a mere Mr. His real name was Alfred Inglis, and he makes his first appearance upon the magical scene at the Egyptian Hall, in London, in 1865. It was Easter Monday, April 17th, of that year when he first rang up his curtain on two Indian tricks—the Mango Tree, and the Indian Basket. He managed to secure the rights of The Sphinx for his 200th performance there, and it at once created a terrific impression. It is not often today that *The Times* has much to say about a magician's performance, but in those days it was different. Different, at any rate, in the case of Stodare and The Sphinx.

This is what *The Times* reported on October 19th, 1865 :—

"Most intricate is the problem proposed by Colonel Stodare, when . . . he presents to his patrons a novel illusion called 'The Sphinx.' Placing upon an uncovered table a chest, similar in size to the cases commonly occupied by stuffed dogs or foxes, he removes the side facing the spectators and reveals a head attired after the fashion of an Egyptian Sphinx. To avoid the suspicion of ventriloquism, he retires to a distance from the figure supposed to be too great for the practice of that art, taking his position on the border-line of the stalls and the area, while the chest is on the stage. Thus stationed, he calls upon the Sphinx to open its eyes, which it does—to smile, which it does also, though the habitual expression of its countenance is most melancholy—and to make a speech, which it does also, this being the miraculous part of the exhibition. Not only with perspicuity, but with something like eloquence, does it utter some twenty lines of verse; and while its countenance is animated and expressive, the movement of the lips, in which there is nothing mechanical, exactly corresponds to the sounds articulated.

"This certainly is one of the most extraordinary illusions ever presented to the public. That the speech is spoken by a human voice there is no doubt, but how is a head to be contrived, which, being detached from anything like a body, confined in a case, which it completely fills, and placed upon a bare-legged table, will accompany a speech, that apparently proceeds from its lips, with a strictly appropriate movement of the mouth, and a play of the countenance that is the reverse of mechanical? . . . Colonel Stodare presents us with a Sphinx that is really worthy of an Oedipus."

The gentleman from *The Times* certainly appears to have been baffled, as many thousands who came to consult Colonel Stodare's Sphinx were baffled for years after. Still are baffled, for the matter of that, for you'll see The Sphinx, or something like it, exhibited on fairgrounds today, as well as occasionally in the programmes of stage illusionists.

Mirrors did it. Mirrors in the plural, this time.

The table had three legs, and was placed on the stage with one leg towards the audience and two legs at the back. The stage setting had curtains at the back and the sides, all of the same material. The table was set equidistant from the side and back curtains. A sheet of plate-glass mirror filled in the space between the front leg and the back leg on each side, and reflected the side-curtains, which appeared to be the curtains at the back. In the secret V-shaped cavity formed by the mirrors, sat an assistant, with his head made up and wigged in imitation of a Sphinx. When the box was placed on the table, and before it was opened, the assistant popped his head through a trap in the table and a corresponding trap in the bottom of the box. He then signalled to the magician by a tap on the underside of the table-top that he was in place, and the front of the box was opened. From then on it was merely a case of the assistant taking up his cue each time he was asked a question.

Some performers have added touches of realism to this famous old illusion, such as having a dummy head in the box. This is taken out and openly displayed before the assistant puts his head into the box. The box is then closed, the assistant reaches into it with his hand, pushes the dummy head to the back of the box, where it is concealed by a flap, and then inserts his own head in its place.

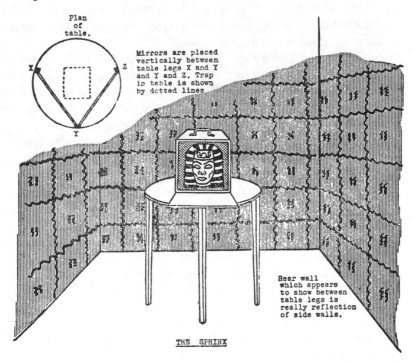

Plan of table.

Mirrors are placed vertically between table legs X and Y and Y and Z. Trap in table is shown by dotted lines.

Rear wall which appears to show between table legs is really reflection of side walls.

THE SPHINX

Stodare himself had one fine clinching effect. He would close the box after the oracle of the Sphinx had spoken, and would then bring the box down to the footlights. The assistant, of course, would have withdrawn his head and closed the traps before this was done. Stodare would rap on the box, and ask the Sphinx if it was still within.

And the Sphinx would answer him!

Stodare, though, was a fine ventriloquist, and it was his voice that answered from "within" the box.

The Sphinx, under various names, and with different make-up, travelled the world in no time. Tobin sold the secret to a waxworks proprietor in Paris, who exhibited it as "The Decapitated Speaker." It was a gruesome exhibition he put on. In the midst of a tableau showing the executioner of the Red Terror at work, the table with the head upon it was sited in a musty cellar. It would describe its own decapitation, to the chilled thrills of the spectators.

Odd, isn't it, how Pepper and his works started this vogue for the morbid? Ghosts, mummies, corpses, executions, all seemed indispensable for a mirror illusion.

The Sphinx had a sister pretty soon. She, too, leaned towards the morbid. Her name was "She," and the plot around her was taken straight from Rider Haggard's novel of the same name. You may remember that "She" was a Greek of considerable charm and perpetual youth, who kept herself young by bathing in the mystic fire of Kor. And then one day, the spell was broken, and instead of restoring her youth, the flames simply burnt her up.

In the illusion, She, the stage setting was much the same as for The Sphinx. A three-legged table stood between curtains, with a curtain of the same material behind. A girl dressed as Rider Haggard's character stood upon the table, and an asbestos canopy was lowered round her, completely concealing her from the audience. Flames and smoke would then pour out from beneath the canopy. The girl would scream. The canopy was lifted, and what was left upon the table? Just what you'd expect —ashes. But a skull would be sitting there among the ashes. Which proved, of course, that the girl had been burnt. Or so it was meant to prove.

Again—The Sphinx.

The girl would descend through a trap in the table-top and would then be hidden by the V-shaped cavity made by the two mirrors. To be quite safe, she would make her exit through the back curtains, after placing the skull and ashes in place on the table-top. Then a magnesium wire inside the asbestos canopy would be ignited—today we'd do it by remote control through a fusing wire—and poor She would have gone up in smoke and screams.

Sometimes the table would have a candelabrum hanging beneath it—"just to prove that there was no hiding place under the table." But this was a touch of sheer nonsense, for who ever heard of a table with candles burning under it? When this was used, two candles would appear to be four because of their reflections in the two mirrors.

If you decide to present "She," please, please, don't hang candles under the table! It's asking for trouble! Let the apparently innocent table speak for itself.

It does seem, doesn't it, as though death and mutilation in one form or another must attend these mirror illusions? In the next one I want to describe, a living head, without a body, is seen resting on a sword placed across the arms of a throne.

The throne has upon its seat a mirror, lying face down and hinged to the frame of the chair at its rear edge. The back of the mirror, which is apparently the seat of the throne, is covered with material to match the seat of the chair.

The lower edge of the chair-back is a trap door, hinged so that it opens forward. The mirror can be raised so that its front edge is on a level with the arms of the chair. It locks in this position, and its upper edge is concealed by the sword laid across the chair arms. The girl makes her entry through the back of the chair, via the trap, and rests her chin on the mirror's edge. The mirror reflects the seat of the chair, which is made of the same material as the back of the chair. And so you believe you're looking through, under the sword, to the back of the chair.

The one important factor in presenting the Decapitated Princess is to be sure that the girl's body and legs, trailing out through the back of the chair, aren't seen. There aren't many chairs on the market that have a girl's body and legs built on to the back, and so it's just possible that if the audience could see these accessories, they might think it a bit odd. Well, I would, anyway.

So watch the angles if you're staging the Decapitated Princess. Watch them, too, if you're seeing the illusion as a spectator. You might be surprised.

THE   DECAPITATED   PRINCESS

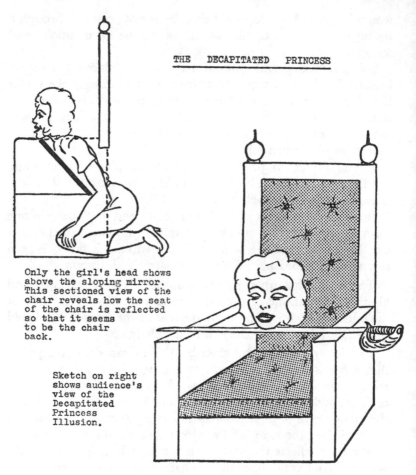

Only the girl's head shows
above the sloping mirror.
This sectioned view of the
chair reveals how the seat
of the chair is reflected
so that it seems
to be the chair
back.

Sketch on right
shows audience's
view of the
Decapitated
Princess
Illusion.

But by now I doubt if anything will surprise you. In fact, about the only surprise you're liable to receive after reading about mirror illusions is to be told that *some* illusions are performed without mirrors.

They are, you know. Nearly all of them. And so—please think twice before you leave the theatre confiding to your friends that "It's all done with mirrors." The chances are that the illusionist you've just seen isn't using mirrors. They're too expensive, **too** heavy to carry about—and too costly to insure.

Chapter Five

THE LADY VANISHES

S<small>HE FIRST</small> vanished from the stage of the little Eden Theatre, in Paris, one spring evening in 1886. A darkly-bearded magician, with a wild, rolling eye, ushered her courteously into a comfortable chair, flung a silken cloth over her, and . . . she vanished.

She—and her descendants—have been vanishing gracefully ever since. Today it might be the suave, smiling Robert Harbin who casts the spell that causes her to disappear. The gilt chair has become a glass cabinet, brilliantly lit. But whoever the magician is, and whatever setting the scene may have, the lady vanishes. She vanishes quickly or slowly, silently or with a double-forte fanfare of brass, in mid-air or firmly secured to the ground. But she vanishes.

And even after seventy and more years, the audience hasn't a clue. It's impossible, but it happens.

How?

It's hardly likely that you'll ever see the original Vanishing Lady Illusion performed these days, so let's do the next best thing, and read the contemporary newspaper account of the original trick. Charles Bertram, the society conjurer, acquired the English rights of the illusion, *L'Escamotage en Personne Vivante,* from the inventor, Buatier de Kolta, within weeks of that first performance in Paris. On August 16th, 1886, he presented it at Maskelyne's Theatre in the Egyptian Hall, London. Next day, the *Morning Post* came out with this account of the illusion that has since baffled millions :—

"Then comes the great event of the evening, *L'Escamotage en Personne Vivante.* Mr. Bertram takes a large newspaper, which he unfolds in the centre of the stage, to cut off any communication with any possible trap door. On this newspaper he places a chair. In the chair he places a young lady, who crosses her hands in her lap over her lace handkerchief.

"After she has apparently been rendered insensible by inhalation, Mr. Bertram produces an enormous black silk handkerchief, about five feet wide by seven feet long. This he brings down to the audience to show that it is not in any way prepared, and the spectators can see that the silken stuff is thin enough to be translucent. With this flimsy shawl Mr. Bertram completely covers the young lady, carefully adjusting it to the floor, and as carefully tying it behind her head.

"When all has been done regularly and in order, and there is only to be seen the figure of the young lady as she sits in the chair enshrouded in the black veil, Mr. Bertram suddenly snatches away the silken shawl, which disappears from his hands at once.

"The young lady has vanished, the chair stands there empty, save that on the seat there remains the lace handkerchief she had held in her fingers; it has fallen from the touch of a vanished hand. Amid the applause which this strange disappearance calls forth, Mr. Bertram steps to the door at the side of the stage and leads on again the young lady who *vient de disparaitre*.

"It is announced that the illusion is performed by Mr. Bertram in London precisely as it is performed by the inventor in Paris; but this is not absolutely exact, as there are two or three modifications in the trick as shown at the Egyptian Hall, which are obvious improvements. The administration of a strange elixir to the young lady about to vanish does not take place in Paris. And in Paris, when the lady vanishes, she does not leave her lace handkerchief on the chair from which she has disappeared. These are both excellent touches of art, admirably adapted to heighten the final effect."

Well, that's what the *Morning Post* reporter saw. He reported it exactly. Can you guess how it was done, this amazing illusion?

If it hadn't been for that newspaper spread out on the stage under the chair, you'd almost certainly have guessed that the lady vanished through a trap in the floor.

And you'd have been quite right.

The touch of isolating the chair from the floor by laying down an ordinary newspaper was the touch of genius. For the newspaper threw off suspicion entirely, making nonsense of the theory that "It's all done with trap-doors."

The newspaper itself, of course, had a trap-door in it, coinciding exactly with a trap in the stage. Two marks on the stage registered precisely with two marks on the paper when it was laid in the right position.

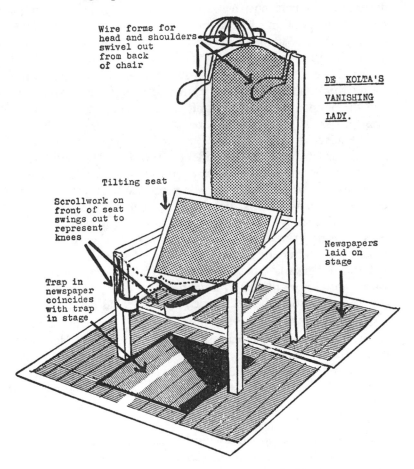

Wire forms for head and shoulders swivel out from back of chair

DE KOLTA'S VANISHING LADY.

Tilting seat

Scrollwork on front of seat swings out to represent knees

Newspapers laid on stage

Trap in newspaper coincides with trap in stage

The chair itself, while appearing quite ordinary, was very much faked. The seat was hinged at the back, so that the lady slid off easily through the trap-door when she drew the bolt that tipped the seat forward. Behind the chair-back was a wire framework representing the lady's head and shoulders. This was hinged, so that when the large silk shawl was held up in front of the chair momentarily, the framework was swung forward by a slight pull on a cord—again operated by the lady.

At the front of the chair was some decorative scrollwork, which opened on hinges and took the place of the lady's knees when she was covered by the cloth. The framework and the dummy knees held out the shape of the silk shawl, which was secured in position. Meanwhile, the lady had shot silently through the newspaper trap and the stage trap, to a platform about three feet below stage level. There she stood and quickly replaced the seat of the chair, which locked in position with a spring catch. This done, her below-stage platform was lowered, and she popped right out of sight, closing the stage trap in readiness for the disclosure of the vanish.

The silken shawl was vanished up the magician's sleeve. A strong cord, running over pulleys, drew it out of sight in an instant, when the conjurer threw wide his arms at the finale.

De Kolta's Vanishing Lady was probably the most showy and baffling illusion that had been produced until that time. Many of us think that it was the best *ever*. So simple in plot and effect. So surprising in its rapid climax. So baffling when one came to puzzle it out after the show.

Other magicians thought so, too. Within a week or so, ladies were vanishing right, left and centre. From stages in all parts of the world they disappeared twice nightly, and at every matinee.

In America, Alexander Herrmann had his mechanics building apparatus to vanish ladies as soon as he heard of de Kolta's triumph. One of his craftsmen, William E. Robinson, eventually produced an illusion in which the lady vanished from the chair, *but the chair had been hoisted into mid-air before she went.* That was later, however, for those industrious ladies continued to vanish for many years.

One of Herrmann's first—and most spectacular—Vanishing Lady illusions was known at different times as "Vanity Fair," and "After the Ball."

On the stage stood a giant-sized pier glass in a frame. The lower edge of the mirror was two or three feet from the ground. It was a solid mirror—no doubt about that—and Herrmann would show it all round to prove it. In front of the mirror, and raised about eighteen inches from the lower edge of the glass, was a small shelf. A short ladder would be provided when the mirror had been shown to be solid, and up this would climb Madame Adelaide Herrmann, who would stand on the shelf, admiring herself in the mirror.

Herrmann would then place a narrow screen around her, but at all times the audience could see the edges of the mirror at top, bottom and both sides. There was no chance of Madame Herrmann dodging round the side when the screen was manipulated round her. She did indeed remain standing on her shelf until . . . she vanished.

Now just how could it be possible for a living woman to disappear under these circumstances? Let's recap. She was positively standing on the shelf after the screen was placed round her. The mirror was of solid, heavy plate-glass. She did not pass round the edges of the mirror, either at the sides or at top or bottom. She'd have been seen if she'd emerged from behind the screen.

That leaves only one solution, doesn't it?

She went through the mirror.

That shelf, with its supporting brackets, hid the secret. The shelf ran the full width of the mirror—five feet. The shelf was supported by two vertical brackets, which were flush with the frame. The top frame of the mirror was about eighteen inches deep, with heavy carved decoration. The glass itself was in two portions, with the shelf and brackets hiding the joint.

The strip of mirror *below* the shelf measured eighteen inches by five feet, and was seen all the time. That piece of glass remained stationary. The upper part moved, sliding into the eighteen-inch top frame.

How, then, was the audience prevented from seeing the glass sliding up? Remember that the small screen didn't hide the sides or the top and bottom of the glass.

The answer is that the audience *did* see the top half of the glass moving—but didn't realise that it was moving. Provided the actual edge of the glass isn't seen, you can't see movement when glass is shifted.

What about the eighteen-inch gap there must have been at the sides of the screen when the mirror went up? That was hidden by a clever stratagem. The top mirror slid down *behind* the lower mirror, and it had a square hole cut in its lower edge. Thus, when the screen was in place, the mirror was raised, and the square hole was exposed in the middle of the step. It was through that hole that Madame Herrmann made her exit, aided

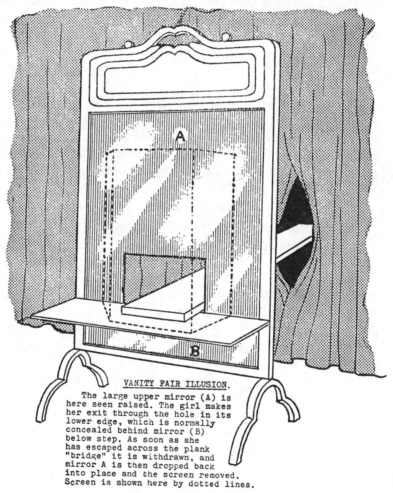

VANITY FAIR ILLUSION.

The large upper mirror (A) is here seen raised. The girl makes her exit through the hole in its lower edge, which is normally concealed behind mirror (B) below step. As soon as she has escaped across the plank "bridge" it is withdrawn, and mirror A is then dropped back into place and the screen removed. Screen is shown here by dotted lines.

by a plank slid through the backcloth to the step. The screen covered the hole at all times. When the lady was safely out of the way, the top mirror was lowered, and the screen was removed.

The mirror was then spun round to show that the lady was not hiding behind it.

Speed and timing, as much as technical invention and execution, make for the success of such illusions. I doubt whether any members of Herrmann's audience ever noticed that for a few seconds the mirror was within four or five feet of the backcloth. It had been wheeled upstage, downstage, it had been turned to show the back—always there was movement, sometimes with two or three things happening at the same time. The result was that the eye could only take in a certain amount—and all eyes were on the lady. The apparent careless placing of the mirror near to the backcloth would go unnoticed. In any case, it would only remain there for a few seconds—just long enough for the mirror to be raised like a window and for Adelaide Herrmann to slip through and across the plank bridge through the back curtain. Then it would be whipped to the front of the stage for the spin round.

I wonder what present-day illusionists would think about travelling with several hundredweight of plate glass which is to be used for just one illusion, lasting a minute or so. Kalanag, of course, carries much heavier equipment than that. His setting and apparatus for the Vanishing Motor Car must fill a railway truck. But few magicians could afford to carry such a weight of props today—even if there were the theatres left to offer them engagements.

A year or two later, Herrmann staged a more direct, simple Vanishing Lady illusion—W. E. Robinson's "Gone!" By then, Robinson had joined Alexander Herrmann as his principal mechanic, and one of the illusions he built was his famous "Gone!" A few years after, when Robinson came to Europe as Chung Ling Soo, he built another "Gone!" for his own show.

"Gone!" is the illusion where a girl sitting on a chair is hoisted six or seven feet into the air. The magician fires a pistol at her, she screams, the pieces of the chair fall to the ground, and the girl is—Gone!

The chair is hoisted by a winch mounted in a scaffold framework. In the top bar of the frame are two pulleys, through which the ropes pass to the winch. Across the middle of the frame is another bar, apparently for strengthening the framework, but really to hide an important part of the mechanism.

The backcloth used for "Gone!" is black. Behind the middle bar on the framework is a kind of roller blind, connected to the top bar by powerful springs. When the catch of the blind is released, the blind—black, to match the backcloth—shoots up to the top bar. The girl is sitting on a loose seat hooked to the ropes. By pressing a catch on this, she disengages the collapsible chair, which falls in pieces to the stage.

The girl in "Gone!" has three things to do—release the catch of the roller blind, which is at once snatched up in front of her, hiding her completely; press the catch that breaks the chair into pieces; and—hold tight!

In one version of "Gone!" one of these operations is carried out by an assistant who helps to carry the scaffolding on to the stage. He stands leaning against the side of the framework, with one hand apparently supporting him. It is this hand that presses the catch which releases the black concealing blind. In that case, the girl can concentrate on holding tight and letting the bits of chair fall.

"Gone!" remained a popular illusion for many years. After Alexander Herrmann died, Harry Kellar, another famous American illusionist, took it over and presented it all over the U.S.A.

Even today you'll find veteran music-hall enthusiasts who talk with wonder of "The girl who vanishes in front of your eyes— no covering, no screen, nothing. She simply vanishes!"

That, really, was the trouble with the Vanishing Lady. The plot was too simple. It wasn't long before audiences knew what to look for, either. When a lady was escorted on to the stage, seated in a chair, and "hypnotised," they knew just what was going to happen—even though they didn't know *how* it would happen.

Maskelyne and Devant changed all that. They probably vanished more ladies from their stages than were ever recorded in the Missing Persons Bureaux anywhere in the world. But they gave the ladies a sound reason for their disappearance, and so made the illusion even more mystifying. If you don't know exactly when the lady's going to vanish, then her sudden and

inexplicable disappearance becomes all the more effective. It's
over before you have time to think: "Now I'll watch this bit
carefully. This time I really *will* find out where she goes!"
Before you can say: "There she goes!"—she's gone!

Devant's famous "Mascot Moth" illusion set the theme for
the story-plots that came in a steady succession over the years.
The idea for the theme of the Mascot Moth story came to David
Devant in a dream, in which he found himself chasing a moth
about the stage. The moth was a winged human being, and
Devant dreamed that he was trying to tempt it towards him,
when its wings shrivelled in a candle flame and the moth disappeared.

He awoke from the dream in the middle of the night, and sat
up planning the playlet he later produced so many times on
the stage.

It was days later that the solution to his problem—how to
vanish the moth?—came to him. The method was diabolically
ingenious. The girl playing the part of the moth wore a special
dress which could be supported, and which could hold its shape
with no girl inside it. When the girl stood in a certain spot on
the stage, a tube was brought up through the floor behind her.
In a secret pocket of the dress was a reel of strong cord, and the
magician would, at one point of the illusion, drop this reel down
the tube. Below stage, a man would catch the reel and thread the
cord over two widely-spaced pulleys, so that it could be instantly
twitched down the tube at the right moment.

The girl's dress carried two large wings, and these she joined
together before her face just before the vanish. When her face
was covered, she gave three taps on the floor, which was the
signal to a stage-hand operating a bracket lift on which she stood.
The stage-hand would turn a windlass which gently lowered the
square of flooring, taking the girl down with it. Once the girl
was down, and the trap replaced, the man controlling the cord
would give it a strong pull, and the self-supporting dress—now
empty, of course—would be snatched down through the tube
more speedily than the eye could follow its movement.

What of the tube itself, projecting there above the stage? That
was covered by the magician, who stood between it and the
audience. The moment the dress had been twitched down the

tube, the tube itself would be lowered, and the stage would be "clean." The magician could stand back. The girl and her moth costume would have been snatched out of sight—and another lady had vanished!

This series of operations was over in a moment. It was divided into three phases. First, the girl was lowered gently but quickly down on the small silent lift. Then the dress was pulled down the tube. And finally the tube itself was withdrawn. Between phases one and two it was possible for the magician to move about freely, as so far there was no suspicion in the minds of the audience. To their minds, the girl was still there. They could see her costume moving gently where she stood—and how could the costume be there without the girl? But when the time came to make the costume disappear, the magician had to stand close to it to conceal the tube standing five feet above floor level.

Again, timing and speed gave illusion to the illusion.

Remember that, please, when the thought occurs to you: "Oh! Mechanical stuff! I could do that!"

One fraction of a second out, and there's no illusion. Four people were concerned in making that girl disappear. Months of work had gone into the making of the plans and the construction of the apparatus, which was the work of Henry Bate, of Brighton, that famous builder of magical properties. Weeks of rehearsal had polished the illusion to the finished gem it became. The envanishment occupied only seconds of time, but the work put into it represented many hundreds of man-hours, to use the current jargon.

If a stage-hand working on the Mascot Moth had sneezed at the critical moment; if a splinter of wood on the stage had fouled the tube as it descended; if Devant had been six inches out in his placing a split second before the dress vanished—it would have been the illusion that vanished, instead of the lady. But never once, in the hundreds of times he showed the Mascot Moth, was there a hitch. Each performer and each stage-hand did his work perfectly every time. That was the standard David Devant always aimed at—and always achieved.

The self-supporting costume and its vanish down a tube were used in other similar illusions, notably "The Magician's Heart" and "The Artist's Dream."

In the latter, the girl who is to vanish steps out of a picture painted by the magician, who plays the part of an artist asleep in his studio. The late Julian Wylie, famous impresario of the early years of this century, gave Devant the idea of using the tube vanish in the Artist's Dream, which became one of Maskelyne and Devant's show pieces for many years after. When David Devant died, Cecil Lyle bought the apparatus for the Artist's Dream, and added an improving touch or two to its presentation. Lyle would stand between the girl and the tube, with the girl nearer to the audience. The costume would go down the tube *over Lyle's shoulder.*

There was a drawback to this, however. If a stage-hand was a little slow, the audience could see the dress vanish, and more than once I've heard people in the theatre whisper: "The dress has gone into his costume!" So it appeared, too. That, though, is one of the risks an illusionist takes when he tours from theatre to theatre. In the case of Maskelyne and Devant's, the show was resident in one theatre for many years, and the stage staff were as much members of the company as were the artists themselves.

You'd think that, despite all the ingenuity usually shown by illusionists, nothing new could be added to the Vanishing Lady illusion, once a perfect vanish had been achieved. That's what the magicians thought, too, until—Devant made a girl vanish *in the middle of the orchestra stalls.*

"Beau Brocade" was the title of the sketch, which was more than a Vanishing Lady illusion. It was one of the forerunners of that wonderful baffler, The Substitution Trunk Mystery. A girl vanished in full view of the audience, to be found a second later locked in a previously examined "empty" trunk. The substitution in this case involved a little cheating, though, for the girl in the trunk was not the girl who disappeared. She was her twin sister. The mechanism for showing the trunk empty and then getting her into it doesn't concern us in this chapter. Let's just say it was a trick trunk and leave it at that, shall we?

But you'll want to know, I'm sure, how it was possible to make a girl vanish into thin air from the middle of the stalls. The answer is—it isn't possible. But many hundreds of spectators who saw Beau Brocade will hotly deny that statement. They are wrong, of course. They only *thought* they saw the girl in the stalls.

Here's how it happened. First, the trunk was shown empty and securely fastened up again. Then a large cloth was displayed and laid on the stage. The girl was "hypnotised" and placed in the middle of the cloth, reclining gracefully. Two assistants took the cloth by the four corners and lifted the girl with it, thus bringing her down to the footlights. The girl could be seen lying there as the cloth was wrapped round her. Then Devant picked up the heavy bundle and walked down the steps into the audience with it. Someone sitting in the stalls—it might have been you! —was invited to make sure the girl was in the bundle, and was asked to take hold of her. Just as he did so, the cloth would collapse—empty.

That's what the audience saw. What they didn't see was the substitution of an inflated rubber dummy for the girl lying on the cloth. It was this bundled-up dummy that was carried down to the audience, and on a touch from the magician, it collapsed, and the cloth was waved and thrown back to the stage. There, of course, it was out of reach of that inquisitive member of the audience—yes, it might have been you?—who would have liked to examine it.

The substitution came when the two assistants were lifting the four corners of the cloth to pick it—and the girl—up. First they lifted the front corners, which momentarily concealed the girl. As they did so, the girl rolled quickly on to a pivot trap just behind the rear edge of the cloth. The trap turned, depositing her in a hammock below the stage. On the under side of the trap was the inflated dummy, which was scooped on to the cloth and partly wrapped up, being firmly attached to the cloth so that it and the cloth would not part company later. The dummy had a wax mask made from the girl's features, and the wig the audience saw was an exact counterpart of the white wig they'd seen the girl wearing, as Beau Brocade.

And so what was carried down into the audience was no girl, but a mask, a wig, several square feet of thin rubber, and about 20 pounds per square inch of compressed air!

Buatier de Kolta, first magician to make a lady vanish, must

have been amazed, as time went on, at the variations illusionists
my explanation of it is the truth.
played upon his theme. And one of the most amazing of all was
undoubtedly the illusion known as "Asrah," invented by Servais
Le Roy in the 1890s.

Asrah combined two illusions—the Floating Lady and the
Vanishing Lady. First, the girl apparently floated in mid-air;
then—she vanished.

Le Roy was a Belgian magician who spent most of his life in
England and America. "Le Roy, Talma and Bosco" was the title
of his act, and a fine act it was. Le Roy was the illusionist and
magician; Talma, his lady partner, was billed as "The Queen
of Coins"; and Bosco was the clown of the trio. There were,
incidentally, several Boscos, in succession, and the part may be
looked on as having been a sound training school for conjurers
who later became famous, just as the job of Julius Zancig's
partner (before Mrs. Zancig came into the act) trained more
than one of today's leading magicians.

Asrah, according to Servais Le Roy, was born in the early
1890s, on the stage of the Circle Theatre, Columbus Circle,
New York. It was early morning by the time the equipment was
ready for operation, and Le Roy stationed Leon Bosco and
an assistant in the auditorium to watch the illusion from the
audience's point of view. Despite their commendations, Le Roy
never felt confident in the illusion. After the first test demonstration before this audience of two, he broke up the apparatus
and wrote it off as chargeable to experience.

But three years later, pressed by Bosco, Le Roy built the
illusion afresh, and staged it at the Empire Theatre in Johannes-
burg, South Africa. "Asrah made her appearance before an
enthusiastic public and a somewhat doubtful performer," said
Le Roy afterwards.

It almost seems a shame to set down on paper the secret of
Asrah, even though this won't be the first description to appear
in print. The trouble is, you're pretty sure to swear that such an
illusion wouldn't deceive *you*. Neither would it—if you knew in
advance what the secret was. But believe me, Asrah has deceived,
and continues to deceive, many thousands of theatre audiences.
And the next time *you* see it performed, you won't believe that

Which is just as it should be, although *I* wouldn't deceive you for worlds!

All right, then. Let's first watch Asrah from the stalls. The magician leads on his lady assistant. He hypnotises her. She falls, rigid, into the arms of an assistant, who places her on an open table, well upstage. A silken cloth is flung over her, and beneath the cloth she is seen to rise slowly into the air. Waveringly, the horizontal body rises until it is out of reach of the illusionist, who can just reach the edge of the silken cloth. He takes the last corner of the cloth in his hand as the body floats still higher, and twitches the cloth.

It falls to the ground, empty and unprepared, and—the Lady's Vanished!

No body floats in the air where a moment ago the hypnotised girl had been suspended invisibly. Now she's *truly* invisible!

At this point, you're probably suspecting that the girl must be hidden in the top of the table, but . . . there's no table to be seen on the stage by now! Well, it's your own fault. You weren't watching the assistants when they wheeled the table off into the wings! You were too busy watching the girl floating up there beneath the cloth.

Again, that's exactly as it should be! You're too late now to check your suspicions by taking a good look at that table through your opera glasses! It was there for you to see plainly before, though, so you go home thinking that surely, after all, the table couldn't have been tricked.

You're wrong again, of course.

The table hides the secret—or rather half the secret—of Asrah. When it was wheeled quietly and unobtrusively away by the assistants, it carried with it the girl. This you'll not believe when you see Asrah performed next time. The table, you'll say, was far too thin to conceal the girl. Why, the edge of it, including decoration and fancy mouldings, was no more than four inches thick.

True enough. Four inches thick—*at the edge*. But if you'd been able to get right up to that table, you'd have seen that the centre of the table was cunningly raised, and that the edge ran away to a four-inch bevel. The thickness of the table in the middle is more like eight or nine inches, but this added width isn't noticed because you, in your stall or dress circle seat, have only one viewpoint. You can't move about and compare one aspect of the table with another. Decoration helps to hide the extra thickness, too.

The middle of the table top is made of rubberized cloth slats, through which the girl can slip into the hollow top.

Very well. The girl is hidden in the table top. *Then what is it that rises under the cloth?*

Please don't be disappointed when you hear that it's a wire shape.

And if you ask me why the wire shape is invisible when the cloth is twitched away, I'll advise you to examine the pattern of the background more closely. Usually, a complicated background pattern is best for Asrah, as the wire shape is then hidden completely against the complexities of the pattern. Also, cunning use of the lighting, at the point where the "girl" vanishes, will render this wire shape quite, quite invisible—from where you're sitting.

I'm sure you won't need me to tell you that the wire shape is hidden behind the rear edge of the table at the start of the show, and that the girl swings it into place as she sinks into the table top. Two fine cords, running through pulleys above the stage, and manipulated by a man in the wings, serve to raise the cloth-covered shape into the air.

But, as I said, you simply won't believe that this explanation of Asrah is the right one next time you see it performed. And I'm glad of it!

One of the most technically perfect Vanishing Lady illusions was perfected by Jasper Maskelyne at his St. George's Hall Theatre in London—The Dizzy Limit. To my mind it was flawless both in conception and execution. And so it still is, in the version performed by Robert Harbin today on stage and television.

In The Dizzy Limit, the magician has a hammock made of openwork cordage, which he exhibits to show its transparency and complete freedom from trickery. The hammock is swung about five feet above floor level, and several feet clear of the sides of the stage and the backcloth. The girl climbs into it— there's no doubt about that; she really *does* climb into it. The magician fires a pistol at her (or, in the case of Harbin, makes a magnificently magical gesture) and—she's gone!

The hammock's there, swinging idly. The girl's wrap is there, fluttering to the ground. But there's no girl!

Bob Harbin has another spectacular Vanishing Lady illusion, which is the very last and latest word in such things. I don't expect to see an improvement on *this* one until a real, genuine, spell-casting wizard comes along. Even then, I don't think he'll do more than just make somebody vanish!

Harbin's latest Vanishing Lady has this about it : *it's a lady from the audience who is made to vanish.* Imagine that! No confederate. No trained lady assistant. No skilled lady magician. Just a lady—*any lady*—from the audience.

Harbin lectures, briefly but accurately, on modern electronic developments. The curtains part, and there in the middle of the stage, well down towards the footlights and twenty feet clear of anything that might afford concealment, is a large glass cabinet. The lady from the audience is handed in by a door at the back of the cabinet, and lights are switched on inside it. There she stands, brightly illuminated, in full view behind the glass front, and without any atom of concealing material.

The stage lights dim, Harbin's electronic machine goes into action, and slowly, gradually, but plainly—the Lady Vanishes. Until . . .

She has really and truly vanished.

What's more, she'll stay vanished until Harbin reverses the switch on his machine. This, however, he does (although he tells me that one day he intends to throw the switch and walk out of the theatre—just to see what happens), and by degrees, inch by inch the lady reappears. First she's a shadowy wraith, a mere suggestion of an outline, here one second and gone the next. Then she seems to flicker at the edges as she takes on a bolder form. Then she's back with us once more.

And as she comes smilingly out of the cabinet and resumes her seat in the audience, *she hasn't a clue as to what's happened to her.* While she was invisible in the cabinet, she was invited to call out, to prove that she was still there. She called out. She was invited to look into a mirror held before the cabinet. She looked—*and couldn't see herself.*

Harbin's cabinet has done some peculiar things in its time. I remember one Magic Circle show when the lady didn't reappear! Instead, there appeared in the cabinet the figure of Claude Chandler, the show's compère. That took quite a bit of unravelling, I can promise you! And the expression on Robert Harbin's face showed that he was more baffled than any member of the audience!

Another time, instead of the lady reappearing at once, a skeleton came to view in the cabinet. There was a moment or two of anguished fiddling with the panel of controls, and the skeleton disappeared like the smile that was wiped off the magician's face when he first saw the gruesome bones. The lady came back though, both times.

And now I can tell you that a new switchboard, officially approved by experts at Harwell, has rendered such phenomena quite impossible. And so if you, madam, feel any qualms about acting as Harbin's volunteer assistant, you can dismiss them. Get in that cabinet and vanish! You'll reappear, all right.

Let's go back a few years in time now, from the days of Bob Harbin's electronic wonder to the golden days of the bathing machine. This time, the magician is Chris Charlton, a dear old friend, and the most knowledgable wizard of our time. Chris is semi-retired now, but he still keeps his big illusion show in his stores.

Chris, too, used a mid-air vanish for his lady assistant. In the middle of the stage he would have a small model of a bathing machine, just big enough for the girl to climb into.

In she'd get, and pose on the doorstep, hands lightly touching the frame of the door. The bathing machine would be hoisted high above the stage, Chris would cast his spell, the girl would scream, and as the scream faded away, so did the girl. And to torment your imaginative faculties still more, the bathing machine fell to the stage in sections.

There they are. The three outstanding Vanishing Lady illusions of recent years. Each one different in plot, presentation and method. Maskelyne's Dizzy Limit, Harbin's Electronic Cabinet, and Charlton's Bathing Machine.

How were they done, these three?

Did I overlook telling you their secrets? So I did.

And another thing I overlooked was the title of Chris Charlton's bathing machine illusion.

He called it "The Lady Vanishes." Which is just about where we came in, isn't it?

Chapter Six

THE TRICK THAT NEVER WAS

THE INDIAN ROPE TRICK—*that's* The Trick That Never Was. You've never seen it, I've never seen it, and that neighbour of yours, who spent part of the war in India and saw everything else—he's never seen it either.

An Indian Rope Trick, yes. But *the* Indian Rope Trick, no. Stage illusionists have been presenting versions of this legendary miracle for many years, but nobody has yet persuaded any miracle-monger to perform *the* Indian Rope Trick. Not that there's been any lack of inducement. J. N. Maskelyne offered £5,000 to anyone who could do it. The Magic Circle has a standing offer of £1,000 for a sight of the trick. Travellers in the East who wanted to see the trick have offered comparable sums. Houdini, that lavish, bouncing issuer of challenges to the world, backed up his challenge with dollars. The Duke of Windsor's agents (when he was Prince of Wales) scoured the Indies, an open cheque in one hand and a fountain pen and contract in the other, in their efforts to obey H.R.H.'s edict: "Show me the Indian Rope Trick."

The Prince never saw it. Houdini never saw it. Old Man Maskelyne never saw it, and neither did his successors. And the Magic Circle bank account still has that £1,000 on the credit side.

So it looks as though you and I will never see it, money being as tight as it is today.

But however much money you may have, it'll make no difference. You'll never see the Indian Rope Trick in the usual version described by those eager travellers one meets so often.

The reason is simple. The Indian Rope Trick can't be done. That being so, we might as well close this chapter now. But we won't. You'll want to know more about this odd mystery. For there *is* a great mystery here, not so much in the matter of

71

"How's it done?"—because it *isn't* done—but relating to "How did the tale start?"

First, let's listen to a traveller's description of the trick. This is reported verbatim from a talk I had with a man who claimed to have seen the Indian Rope Trick. He was an educated man who'd travelled in India and the East. His account of the trick tallies with most other stories about it. Here it is:—

"I *did* see it! I'm not easily fooled,* as you know. I saw it as plainly as I see you now. It was at Cawnpore, I think, in about 1930. The jadoo wallah (conjurer) came into the compound while we were sitting on the verandah after dinner. He spread a big cloth on the ground and sat in the middle of it and blew on a sort of flute with a bulge like a coconut at the end—you must have seen them; they make a dismal wailing noise.

"That, of course, hypnotised us. Yes, it was the flute that did it, I'm sure.

"Then he unwound a rope from beneath his shirt and said a lot of words over it. Yes, of course I understood most of them, although much of what he said was in dialect. I speak the language pretty well. I forget what they meant. It was years ago, remember.

"Well, he sort of whirled this rope round and round his head, and what with that and the flute thing tootling all the time, it made me pretty dizzy. But not too dizzy to watch, of course.

"He made a big swing with the rope, and threw it up in the air. It stayed there, as stiff as a board."

Here he paused to light a cigarette, puff at it, look at it to make sure it was burning all right—and think out the next bit. I waited, without prompting him.

Then he continued:—

"Yes, up it went, and stayed there. There was a little boy with this chap. I forgot to mention him. And the boy swarmed up the rope as far as he could. The jadoo wallah looked in his bag and took out a damn great knife. He muttered more words over it and threw it up. The boy screamed, and vanished.

---

* He was. The simplest card trick baffled him.

"Later, the jadoo wallah let us all examine the rope and the knife. Quite ordinary, they were.

"The boy? Er . . . Oh yes. The boy came running up from among the crowd later. Yes, it was the same boy.

"My explanation is that we were all hypnotised. The flute thing and the rope whirling about did it. It's well known that you can be mesmerised by that sort of thing."

Well, that's what Mr. X. told me. It's a short tale, but that's only because he knew I was taking it down word for word. At other times this man would ramble on happily for thousands of words to describe the slightest incident. But the notebook and pencil cooled him down, this time.

I didn't question him on his story, but took it home and transcribed it on to the typewriter. Later—weeks later—I asked the man to tell me again about the Indian Rope Trick, which he did willingly. But this time, alas! the site of the miracle had changed. He'd seen it at Delhi, he thought, in the 1920s. This time, there was no flute. This time, the boy came down in a shower of arms and legs and was never seen again. *This* time, there was no notebook, and Mr. X. really went to town with his account of the trick.

For what it's worth, you may like to pick a few holes in Mr. X.'s graphic account of what he saw at Cawnpore (he thought) in 1930 (about).

First: the flute. Try to imagine the conjurer playing his flute and whirling a long rope round his head at the same time. Could you do it? I couldn't. The flute itself, too, is a snake-charmer's flute, and not a conjurer's.

The flute its out of place, but Mr. X. needed it in his story for one reason: to provide the "hypnotism." For he was convinced that the Indian Rope Trick had been seen, but had only been seen by people under the influence of hypnotism.

Then that pause. It was laughably obvious that while he was looking for his cigarettes and going through the performance of lighting one, his brain was working—fast for him, but slowly compared with the normal—on what to say next. An honest witness of anything, who may be in doubt as to his memory of an event, will stop his narrative and concentrate on recalling what happened. He may say something like: "Now wait a moment. I've got to think about this. Give me a minute to collect my thoughts. . . ." A lying witness will pretend to occupy himself with something else while he hurriedly—and with a guilty air—composes his thoughts.

And that's just what Mr. X. was : a lying witness. I suppose that normally he was truthful enough, but when challenged on the subject of the Indian Rope Trick he felt he just *had* to defend the honour of his reputation. He was a teller of travellers' tales. And that's just about what most "witnesses" of the Indian Rope Trick are. Set them against this background and see how they merge into it! The man who's seen the Indian Rope Trick (or says he has) is the man who has other tall stories to tell, as a rule. In time, perhaps he grows to believe his stories. It's a kink with some people, isn't it?

But if I'd believed my Mr. X. the first time he told the tale, could I have believed him the second time?

By then, the locale had changed, the date had changed, and the climax had changed. By then, forgetful Mr. X. had exposed himself as an enthusiastic liar.

He wasn't the first.

According to all the records, one Abu Abdallah Mohammed Ibn Batuta was about the earliest man to come home and say he'd seen the Indian Rope Trick. Ibn Batuta ("The Traveller") lived from 1304 to 1377, and the encyclopedia describes him as "Arab traveller whose writings are of foremost authority on the cultural history of Islam in the post-Mongol period."

All right. Then let's call the witness, Ibn Batuta. Here's *his* deposition, found in an ancient Arabic manuscript written six hundred years ago : —

"I was entertained by the Emir in his own house in a most splendid manner. At the banquet were present the Khan's jugglers, the chief of whom was ordered to show some of his wonders. He then took a wooden sphere in which there were holes, and in these long straps, and threw it up into the air until it went out of sight, as I myself witnessed, while the strap remained in his hand. He then commanded one of his disciples to take hold of and ascend by this strap, which he did, until he also went out of sight.

"His master then called him three times, and no answer came. He then took a knife in his hand, apparently in anger, laid hold of the strap, and also went quite out of sight.

"He then threw the hand of the boy upon the ground, then his foot, then his other hand, then his other foot, then his body, then his head.

"He then came down, panting for breath, and his clothes were stained with blood. The juggler then took the limbs of the boy and applied them one to another. He then stamped upon them and it stood up complete and erect.

"I was astonished, and seized, in consequence, by a palpitation of the heart, but they gave me some drink and I recovered.

"The Mohammedan judge, sitting by my side, swore that there had been neither ascent nor descent, nor cutting away of limbs, but that the whole had been mere juggling."

That's quite a story, by any standard. But the later reporters of the Indian Rope Trick can do better than Ibn Batuta. Without so much as the palpitation of an eyelid, *they* make it happen out of doors.

There's an important difference there. You'll have noticed that Ibn Batuta was entertained to this mystery *in* the Emir's house? Indoors, it would be easy to perform a version of the Indian Rope Trick. The rope—or strap, in this case—had a weight on the end (". . . . a wooden sphere in which there were holes . . ."). That would ensure easy aiming when the strap was thrown upwards. It would also make it simple for an accomplice above to catch it and secure it so that the strap could be climbed.

Even the fact that there was any sort of covering overhead, whether it was roof, ceiling, or even a fabric pavilion, makes the performance feasible and simple. In a theatre, the illusionist usually depends upon his rope being suspended from the flies above. In the Emir's house, the jugglers could have presented the trick in the same manner.

Ibn Batuta may have been a truthful and accurate reporter, although, according to other of his accounts of conjuring performances, he was an impressionable one. But he does seem to have believed in what he saw, or thought he saw.

Which is more than I would say of most of today's "witnesses" of the Indian Rope Trick.

The Rope Trick was too good a trick, or too good a traveller's tale, to be allowed to rest with Ibn Batuta, and no doubt the story of the rigid rope was often told by returning travellers during the years that followed.

A century after Ibn Batuta had been gathered to Paradise, there were unconfirmed reports of the Rope Trick having been presented in Venice. But another hundred years passed, apparently, before anyone thought it worth while to put the Indian Rope Trick on paper again.

Johann Wier, in his *De Prestigiis Daemonum* (Basle, 1566), has a record of the trick, although he does not say whether he saw the performance himself, or whether he had the account of it second-hand. The date is given as 1550, and this is what Messer Wier had to say :—

". . . At Magdeburg a certain magical Juggler, who was wont to lead about a little Horse for show, would let him walk about in a circle in an open Theatre, and at the end of the Show would tell the Company that he could get but little Money among Men, and therefore he would go up to Heaven; whereupon he would throw a Cord up in the Air, and the little Horse would go up it; himself, taking hold of the Horse's Tail, would follow him; his Wife, taking hold of him, would follow also, and a Maid Servant would follow her, and so mount up in the Air, as it were linked together, the Spectators standing in great Admiration; until a certain Citizen, coming by chance that way, and asking what was done, it was answered that a Juggler with his little Horse was gone up into the Air; whereupon he assured them that he saw him just going into an Inn in the Street; therefore, finding themselves deluded, they went away."

And that, it seems, was that. History doesn't relate what happened to the Cord. The Juggler, his Wife, his Maid Servant, and his little Horse having vanished at the top of the Cord, you'd have thought the Company would have seized upon the Cord as evidence of what they'd seen. But no. Finding themselves deluded, they went away.

For all I can say, the Cord is still hanging there in mid-air somewhere in Magdeburg. Here, for once, is no record of what goes up having come down.

The Rope Trick reporters were really getting into their stride now. One notable spectator was the Mogul Emperor Jahangir, who ruled in Delhi from 1605 to 1627. He was the father of Shah Jehan, who built the Taj Mahal at Agra. Jahangir was one of the earliest royal reminiscers, and several manuscripts of his memoirs are in existence. In one of them, Jahangir records a Command Performance by a band of Bengalee jugglers. What do you think was included in their repertoire? Yes. The Indian Rope Trick.

Here is what the Emperor said he saw : —

". . . They produced a chain of fifty cubits [75 feet] in length, and in my presence threw one end of it towards the sky, where it remained as if fastened to something in the air. A dog was then brought forward, and, being placed at the lower end of the chain, immediately ran up, and, reaching the other end, disappeared in the air. In the same manner, a hog, a panther, a lion, and a tiger were successively sent up the chain, and all disappeared at the upper end. At last they took down the chain, and put it into a bag, no one ever discerning in what way the animals were made to vanish into the air in the mysterious manner described. . . ."

Some experts describe this manuscript as being garbled and spurious. I'm not surprised at that.

News got about the world, even in those days. A few years later, a Chinese author, Pu Sing Ling, described a juggler's performance he saw in about 1630.

The juggler, who had a pole over his shoulder and was accompanied by a boy, was asked to produce some peaches. There was snow on the ground, and it wasn't the time of year for peaches. The juggler offered to send up to Heaven for them. Out came the rope, and up it went into the air. The juggler paid it out yard by yard, as though someone up there was pulling it in, and the top end disappeared in the clouds. Just in time, too, according to Pu Sing Ling, for by then the juggler only had a short piece left in his hand. If those clouds had been twenty feet higher, it looks as though there'd have been no Rope Trick for Pu Sing Ling to report.

The juggler's boy swarmed up the rope and vanished into the clouds. A few minutes later, down came a peach "as big as a basin."

But the boy must have been caught robbing the celestial peach orchards, for before you could say "Make mine an apricot," down came bits of boy. Arms, legs, body and head rained down in a gruesome shower. It takes more than a dismembered boy to disturb these jugglers, though, for this one just gathered up the pieces and popped them into his box. And from that box, a few moments later, out came the boy, whole and undamaged.

There's a link with Ibn Batuta here. Pu Sing Ling reports that the trick was done by members of the White Lily sect, a Chinese secret society which had flourished since about 1350. And some of Ibn Batuta's writings suggest that he saw the Rope Trick performed in Hankow, China, just about that time. It's more likely, though, that if Ibn Batuta saw Chinese jugglers, they were travelling performers, working in a Moslem country. He refers to "The Khan's jugglers" in "The Emir's own house." "Khan" is a Mongol title, and "Emir" is the Arabic word for "Prince."

Pu Sing Ling places his version of the mystery out of doors. The nearest Ibn Batuta's version could place it would be in a courtyard, and if ever you've visited a wealthy Moslem's house, you'll know that the courtyard has shade trees. It sometimes, too, has a silken canopy overhead to keep the sun off. It has sufficient "top" to it, in fact, to make a Rope Trick practicable. Pu Sing Ling had only clouds overhead.

But Pu Sing Ling was reminiscing, not reporting. He was writing of something he saw as a boy, many years earlier. His was a "Those-were-the-days" tale, and an impressive one, at that. But I'd have been more impressed if Pu Sing Ling himself had shown some astonishment at what he said he saw. Good old Ibn Batuta at least had a palpitation of the heart and had to be revived with "some drink." Pu Sing Ling probably had one eye on his public and another on his publisher.

And, by the way, let's not confuse Ibn Batuta's Khan with the Grand Khan of Tartary, Kublai Khan, who showed Marco Polo, that other tale-bearing traveller, a trick or two. Kublai Khan died in 1294. Ibn Batuta wasn't born until 1304.

In passing, it seems odd that Marco Polo never saw the Indian Rope Trick. He seems to have seen plenty of other mysterious oddities, but never once does he mention a juggler throwing a rope into the air.

So far, we've heard evidence from an Arabian, a Chinese, and a Mogul Emperor, with a passing word about a Venetian traveller. What about the English? Didn't they see the Indian Rope Trick in those days?

Of course they did. And they've been seeing it—or rather, *telling* about seeing it—ever since.

One Edward Melton, a seaman, came back from Batavia, in the Dutch East Indies, in 1670 with a report of it. A Chinese troupe had performed the Indian Basket Trick, followed by balancing feats with long poles.

"Then," wrote Melton, "one of the same gang took a ball of cord, and, grasping one end of the cord in his hand, flung the other end up into the air with such force that its extremity was beyond reach of our sight. He then immediately climbed up the cord with indescribable nimbleness, and got so high that we could no longer see him, and went out of sight."

Then came the shower of limbs, etc., which were thrown into a basket, from which the complete man emerged.

There's a slight illogicality about Melton's account. Why should the climber have fallen in bits? Nobody had climbed up after him with a knife, and there's no mention of anyone throwing a knife up to him.

In that flaw lies the key to Melton's version of the mystery. *He never saw it happen.* If he had, he'd have rounded off the tale with the account of someone getting at the climber with a knife. His is a typical example of the story we hear today. If the narrator is reminded that he's omitted an essential part, he invariably agrees, and tacks on the missing bit apologetically. He probably makes a mental note not to forget that part of the tale next time he tells it.

But when a man sets down on paper an account of something so ghastly and hair-raising as the Indian Rope Trick and its accompanying dismemberment, he has time to think. He's not likely to let an incomplete version go out—unless he's not telling the truth. And then he just has to rely on his memory of what

someone else has told him. Which is vastly different from seeing
it happen.

Away, then, with Edward Melton, seaman, whose evidence
seems highly suspect. And let's call a more recent witness.

He is Lieutenant F. W. Holmes, V.C., of Bermondsey, who
not only saw the Indian Rope Trick—in part—in India in 1917,
but took a photograph of it, which was reproduced in the
London newspapers two years later, and again in 1934.

This is what Lieut. Holmes wrote :—

"One day in May, 1917, I was standing on the verandah
of my bungalow at Kirkee, near Poona, in the company of
several other officers, when an old man and his boy came up
to us, over the open ground, to give us his performance. He
had no pole—a thing which would have been impossible to
conceal.

"He began by unwinding from about his waist a long rope,
which he threw upwards in the air, where it remained erect.
The boy climbed to the top, where he balanced himself as
seen in the photograph which I took at that moment. He then
descended, and the conjurer, holding the pole with one hand,
tapped it gently with the other, when it collapsed into rope-
like flexibility, and he coiled it round his waist as before."

That's a report we can believe. But if Lieut. Holmes had so
much as hinted that the boy vanished, or that he came down in
a shower of legs and arms, we could have written off his account
as well.

It's an easy matter to construct a flexible pole from short
sections of bamboo, and to disguise it as a rope. The loosely-
coupled pieces ensure that the "rope" is flexible enough at
ordinary times, but a very slight tightening of the connecting
cord serves to make the "rope" rigid enough for a small boy to
climb up it and balance at the top.

And Lieut. Holmes's version puts us on the track of the
veritable Indian Rope Trick. This is the trick that *is* seen. But
how often does the witness embroider his account of it by
bringing in other tricks and mixing them up into one gorgeous
mess! The dismemberment, for example, is a feature of the
Indian Basket Trick, and is a simple matter of substituting a
dummy for a human being at the right moment. The disappear-

ance of the climber is pure fiction. If ever you meet anyone who
reports having seen the Indian Rope Trick complete with disappearance and dismemberment, ask him one question:—

Why can the climber disappear only at the top of the
rope?

If that doesn't bring you an answer, at least it will make the
tale-teller think a bit.

One witness who could have convinced us that the Indian
Rope Trick is practicable would have been that tireless seeker
after the truth, the late John Nevil Maskelyne. But J. N. Maskelyne becomes a witness by default, at least, for he probably made
more efforts than any man to see the Indian Rope Trick.

And he never saw it.

Maskelyne was a great believer in the value of publicity, at
whatever cost. If he could have persuaded just one fakir to
perform the trick just once in the open, with all the bloody and
baffling trimmings, he'd have done it. But although he offered
what were in his day breath-taking sums of money, no fakir ever
came forward with his rope, his boy and his knife.

In his book, *The Fraud of Theosophy Exposed*, J. N. Maskelyne has this to say about his search for the Indian Rope
Trick:—

"A few years ago, my partners and I decided that, if
possible, we would probe this trick to the bottom. We spent
a considerable sum in advertising for information from any
persons who had witnessed the trick. We also offered to pay
£5,000 a year to any juggler who could perform the trick in
London as it had been described.

"A number of people gave us information. Most of them
were persons who knew somebody who had seen it. A few told
us they had seen it, but their descriptions differed, and they
were uncertain about essential points.

"At last we were fortunate in finding a gentleman in
London we had seen the trick on several occasions, and,
fortunately, also, he had some knowledge of conjuring. He
explained the secret.

"He had been stationed for some years at one of the frontier
military posts, and he had noticed that the troupe of Indian
jugglers always arrived at the time of day when the sun was

in one position and its rays were so strong that Europeans could not be exposed to them.

"The audience, said our informant, occupied the balcony of the bungalow, and were sheltered from the sun by an awning. The jugglers brought a coil of what appeared to be a large rope. As they uncoiled it and held it up, it became stiff; it was evidently jointed bamboo with the joints made to lock. It was covered to look like a rope, and it formed a pole about thirty feet long.

"A diminutive boy, not much larger than an Indian monkey, climbed up to the top of the pole and was out of sight of the audience unless they bent forward and looked beneath the awning, when the sun shone in their eyes and blinded them. As soon as the boy was at the top of the pole, the jugglers made a great shouting, declaring he had vanished. He quickly slid down the rope and fell on the ground behind the juggler who held the rope. Another juggler threw a cloth over the boy and pretended that he was dead. After considerable tom-tomming and incantation, the boy began to move, and was eventually restored to life."

J. N. Maskelyne died without having seen anything that even looked like the traditional Indian Rope Trick. So did his son Nevil. Grandson Jasper renewed the challenge offer, and even went to India in search of "the wonderful Indian magic I had heard about ever since I was a small boy."

What did he find?

"I found nothing but fakes and shams," he writes.

This, too, in spite of his offer of £10,000 and £250 a week salary to anyone who would throw a rope in the air, make it stay there, send up a small boy, go after the boy with a knife, cut up the boy, and then restore the boy to life.

This is what Jasper Maskelyne wrote about his search for the Indian Rope Trick, in his book, *Magic—Top Secret*:—

"Hundreds of travellers and ex-Indian residents claim to have seen this done. But I have never seen it done, and no offers of £10,000 and £250 a week while I was in India could produce a fakir who would do it. They simply smiled when I asked about it, as though they could easily do it, but would not be tempted by filthy lucre to display the wonders of their ancient knowledge to a foreigner. Then they hurried back to their daily urgent business of charming pice and annas from the credulous poor of their own illiterate countrymen. No doubt, though slower, it was easier to get rich that way.

"I know that, on two or three occasions, India has been combed to find a man who will perform the Rope Trick before Royalty. Always without success. I fear it has never been performed at all : it is just one of those tales travellers bring home.

"During my career I have received thousands of letters from people purporting to give eye-witness accounts of it, offering the most ingenious explanations of how it might be done, even occasionally offering to perform a Rope Trick . . . but under their own conditions, which usually include black velvet curtains, and myself posted down in the body of the theatre with no opportunity to examine anything at all. They say, when cross-questioned, that this is because the 'atmosphere' is destroyed by the near presence of a sceptic. I dare say it is! In fact, I have no doubt of it.

"I could devise apparatus to perform the Rope Trick myself, with my own lighting, and with onlookers not nearer than the stalls. It would be costly, perhaps not even a commercial proposition, but I could do it.

"But that is not quite the same trick!"

Of course, many magicians have devised apparatus to perform the Indian Rope Trick on a stage. But, as Jasper Maskelyne says, that's not quite the same trick as the one that's been created in myth and legend. Other illusionists have successfully staged the trick out of doors, but under those circumstances, a demonstration of pole balancing has been all they could offer to the spectators. No magician has yet sent a small boy up a rigid rope and caused him to vanish at the top, or to fall to the ground dismembered.

Horace Goldin, that dapper, plump little Russian-American magician, used to present a very fine, fast Rope Trick. His rope mysteriously rose in the air, a boy climbed up it, Goldin fired a shot, and the boy vanished.

This was accomplished by having the rope pulled up by a fine thread. There was a black velvet background to the setting. The rope itself was a substantial one, thick enough to hide a pair of light metal struts. These were hinged at the top end to a point on the rope some feet in the air. They carried black velvet "wings" which opened out when the struts were elevated to a horizontal position.

The "wings" were opened rapidly and silently by the boy, who hooked a ring on his belt on to a projection at the top end of the struts. Goldin fired the pistol when the boy was ready, the boy dropped a few inches down the rope, the struts were extended in a flash by his weight, and the black velvet "wings" shot out at once, with the boy behind them. The "wings" were imperceptible against the black velvet backcloth, thanks to the special lighting of the stage.

After Goldin died, Cecil Lyle operated a stage version of the Indian Rope Trick. Lyle was one of the greatest magical enthusiasts of all time. He did not regard magic as just a lucrative job, but as his life's work. Many an evening have I spent with him in the library of the Magic Circle, combing the shelves for some little-known book that he might have missed reading in the past. Lyle was always learning, and always putting his new knowledge to good use.

The Great Masoni has an excellent version of the Indian Rope Trick which he used to present on the music halls. I am not at liberty to disclose his method, as Masoni still uses it from time to time. It has many features that set it apart as a masterpiece of dramatic magical entertainment.

Yes, magicians know many ways of staging a *kind* of Indian Rope Trick. And it's surprising how many non-magicians, who may have a little mechanical knowledge, forget that fact! Many such laymen are sadly disappointed when they hear that their great invention — "The Indian Rope Trick" — can be done already by several different methods, probably their own included.

More than once the Magic Circle's Occult Committee have received answers to their challenge, only to find, as they expected to find, that the candidate could put on a version of the trick on a stage, but not outdoors.

It was on a night in 1934 that the Magic Circle issued its challenge—the challenge which has not been met in all the years since. The setting of the Occult Committee's meeting was ordinary enough—the old Oxford House Theatre—but the night was the one night in the year when ghostly results might have been expected. The Committee met on April 30th. Ask any student of magic what night *that* is, and you'll learn that the last night of April is none other than Walpurgis Night, when witches are said to foregather for their great ghastly Witches' Sabbath.

In the Chair was the Circle's President, Lord Ampthill, who had been Viceroy of India thirty years earlier, and who might have been expected to know something of the mysteries of that country. Lord Ampthill was an expert amateur magician in his day, and had sought long and patiently, while in India, for a conjurer who would perform the Indian Rope Trick. Perhaps it's needless to say that he never found one.

He opened the meeting by declaring that the Occult Committee were doing a public service by their investigation into a trick which still inspired persistent belief all over the world. As long as the public was capable of being misled in so many ways, he said, popular superstition could not be dead.

Now one popular superstition of that time was the belief that the late Earl Haig had reported having seen the Indian Rope Trick. Those hardy enough to become embroiled in an argument about the Indian Rope Trick would be faced—and floored—with the triumphant statement: "Ah! But what about Haig? *He* saw it!"

But Earl Haig had died in 1928. However, there was a reliable witness to speak for him—Countess Haig. And Colonel R. H. Elliot, Chairman of the Occult Committee, was able to report to that Walpurgisnacht meeting in 1934 that Countess Haig had come forward to say that she had never once, on any occasion, heard her husband mention having seen the Indian Rope Trick. Negative evidence, certainly. But pretty convincing, when you remember how voluble are all the other "witnesses" of the Indian Rope Trick. Earl Haig had never once mentioned it to his wife.

Colonel Elliot surveyed other evidence, for and against the Rope Trick. And then came the famous Challenge.

"If anyone," declared Colonel Elliot, "will come forward and perform the Rope Trick before my Committee, he shall receive

the sum of £500.* We will give him every opportunity of showing his powers, and will endeavour to investigate the matter to
the very bottom."

Well, it was a long meeting. The minutes of that meeting alone
would make a sizeable chapter of any book. But it closed with
the Occult Committee going on record as saying that they
believed the trick was a myth, and that nobody had ever seen
it performed.

And they've said that same thing ever since.

A few days later, there was another meeting, this time the
annual gathering of the British College of Psychic Science.

That meeting, too, heard about the Indian Rope Trick. Dr.
Alexander Cannon talked about it. Not only *talked* about it, but
said he could *do* it.

This is how Hannen Swaffer reported Dr. Cannon's claim in
the *Daily Herald* for Friday, May 11th, 1934 :—

"Given the conditions I require, I can produce the Rope
Trick in the Albert Hall. It is not produced in any way like
our magical friends think.

"I shall require a large quantity of sand from a certain area,
certain lighting as it were from the sun—this I can arrange—
certain heating arrangements. And, under these circumstances,
everybody will see these phenomena."

You'd be right in thinking that the Magic Circle learned of
this with some interest. And I don't suppose there were many
absentees from the meeting on June 9th, 1934, when Dr. Cannon
attended upon the Occult Committee to discuss arrangements.

Mr. Fred Hocking, Secretary of the Committee, told Dr.
Cannon that they were prepared to pay £500 to anyone who
performed the Indian Rope Trick.

This is what Mr. Hocking told the *Daily Telegraph* afterwards :—

"Dr. Cannon laughed at this sum, and asked for the
£50,000 jocularly mentioned by Lord Ampthill. He said he
would require that sum to bring over his yogis. He also said
he would require a shipload of special sand, and to have the
Albert Hall heated to tropical heat.

* Now—1957—£1,000. W. D.

"We asked Dr. Cannon if, supposing we did guarantee the £50,000, he would give us a banker's guarantee to return the money and pay all expenses if he failed to perform the trick, but he refused."

That mention of £50,000, by the way, was first made by Lord Ampthill at the April 30th meeting, when he had jokingly said they might as well offer £50,000 as £500, because the trick was impossible to do. But the challenge sum was £500.

That summer of 1934 saw many people writing to the papers about the Indian Rope Trick, and many magicians gathered generous publicity by being interviewed. Joe Dunninger, the American mentalist, offered to perform the trick for as little as £10 to pay for apparatus. He could do it in Madison Square Garden (New York's Albert Hall), he said.

Others had their photographs taken, wearing turbans and all the Oriental trimmings, sitting most uncomfortably cross-legged beside a stiff rope sticking up in the air in their gardens.

But I haven't heard of one who went through the whole performance, from start to finish, before an audience of witnesses who could tell the world about it.

Besides trying to persuade someone to show them the Indian Rope Trick, the Occult Committee of the Magic Circle have examined vast quantities of evidence from people who claim to have seen the trick. Not one has been convincing.

But these examinations have served a useful purpose. They have brought the legend out into the light. By comparing one piece of testimony with another, the Occult Committee have been able to sift out the fallacies. And the Indian Rope Trick, they have concluded, is just one big fallacy.

Often, it's been found that the evidence of various spectators stems from one common source. Sometimes it's been traced back to one particular person who has later confessed that he's been hoaxing his hearers. And when a "spectator" says that he and the rest of the audience who saw the Rope Trick were hypnotised, then you might as well close the hearing.

It's possible to hypnotise one person. In fact, it's easy. It's even possible to hypnotise several people at the same time in the same audience. But it is *not* possible to hypnotise all the people, all the time, and every time.

If the Indian Rope Trick in its legendary form has never been seen, why do people persist in saying they've seen it? It's a fair question, to which there are several answers.

First, they may have seen one of the many imitations of the trick. But have they seen the boy vanish? Have they seen his dismembered body fall to the ground? Have they seen the rope *thrown* up in the air, to become rigid?

I don't believe they have. They might tack on these details to the story of the trick they saw. Why? Well, I suppose they do it because they think it's expected of them. They've heard the full story from someone else, and they don't care to admit that they saw only a part of it themselves.

Then, of course, the odd spectator may have been hypnotised. In that case, I'd like to hear what the other spectators saw.

There are others who dabble in psychic affairs, and who may believe that the Indian Rope Trick could be done. They're no doubt completely sincere. But I don't believe they've ever seen this mythical mystery. I don't believe they ever will.

And then there is the vast, verbose army of talkers, travellers, boasters, braggarts, and just plain liars. In clubs, canteens, barrack-rooms and bars all over the world you'll meet them. Don't argue with them. Just listen carefully and, if possible, write down something of what they tell you. Then, as long afterwards as possible, ask them to tell you the story again. Compare the two versions. Ask for dates and place-names each time they tell the tale. Ask for the names of other people who were with them at the time. Compare these data when next they tell you about "The Time I Saw The Indian Rope Trick."

You'll catch them out, I'm sure. But be kind to them. Let them have their fun. After all, you don't have to listen to them a third time!

And if some day *you* see the Indian Rope Trick, *you'll* want to tell the world about it. Mind you, not many will believe you.

I shan't, for one.

Chapter Seven

UP IN THE MIDDLE OF THE AIR

IF YOU'VE never seen the Indian Rope Trick, I'm sure you must have seen the next best thing—the Levitation illusion. Isn't that mystifying? Isn't that real magic? Isn't that a patent impossibility?

Of course it is. And yet you've seen it, and can swear to what you've seen. You know as well as the next man that it's impossible to cause a human being to rise slowly into the air and float there without any means of support. But you've seen it happen, and so, impossible as it seems, it can be done.

How?

Well, before we consider that, let's read what two earlier spectators of a levitation have to say. The first witness is our old friend Ibn Batuta, the impressionable Arab who was so floored by the Rope Trick.

Ibn Batuta placed on record the fact that he saw two conjurers perform at the court of the Mogul Emperor in Delhi. One of the conjurers, he writes with breath-taking calmness, "assumed the shape of a cube and rose in to the air, where he remained suspended. The other took off one of his slippers and struck the ground with it, upon which, it rose into the air, and became motionless at a short distance from the cube. He then touched the other's neck, upon which he descended to the ground and reassumed his natural shape."

How about *that* for a mystery? Rising into the air, yes. We've seen that, all right. But assuming the shape of a cube? Even my friend Devano, who is constructed by nature somewhat in the shape of a cube, would never pass as a *genuine* cube. And Ibn Batuta says he saw a cube. Not simply a man shaped like a cube, but a man who "assumed the shape of a cube." In other words, the man became a cube.

It's not for me to explain how Ibn Batuta's Levitation illusion was performed, thank goodness. And so I merely pass on to you what the enthusiastic Arab says he saw. At the same time, I would invite your attention to the bit where he says the slipper struck the cube on the neck. Unfortunately, Ibn Batuta is no longer with us, nor has he been with us these many years. If he had been, I would ask him to tell us where a cube keeps its neck.

Joking apart, there seem to be two explanations for the account of the Mogul Emperor's magicians' levitation act. One: words have been wrongly interpolated in the translation. Two: Ibn Batuta was drunk. In the case of One, anything might have happened, and we shall never know what did happen. As regards Two—I'd have liked to hear what a second witness had to say, both about the levitation, and about Ibn Batuta.

Ibn Batuta's curious cube floated in the Mogul Palace at Delhi somewhere about the year 1350. More than five hundred years later—on December 13th, 1868—there was reported another inexplicable case of levitation. This time it was nearer home, and witnesses said they saw it happen at Ashley House, Victoria Street, London, S.W.1.

The key witness this time was Windham Thomas, Baron Adare, later fourth Earl of Dunraven. Lord Adare was a Guards officer in his early twenties, and besides being a yachtsman, amateur jockey and big-game hunter, was a close friend of one Daniel Dunglas Home.

Now this Mr. Home was a spiritualist medium of great note, whose name is mentioned today either with bated breath or with angry contumely, according to whether you believe in spiritualistic phenomena or not. And his most remarkable achievement was said to be the ability to float in the air. Records of his mysterious levitations are numerous, although, alas! many of them took place in complete darkness or dim light.

Describing that stirring evening of December 13th, Lord Adare wrote:—

"... Home proposed a sitting. We accordingly sat round a table in the small room. There was no light in the room, but the light from the window was sufficient to enable us to distinguish each other, and to see the different articles of furniture. Home went into a trance. ..."

"Home was both elongated and raised in the air. He spoke in a whisper, as though the spirits were arranging something. He then said to us: 'Do not be afraid, and on no account leave your places.' He went out into the passage. . . .

"We heard Home go into the next room, heard the window thrown up, and presently Home appeared standing upright outside our window; he opened the window and walked in quite coolly. . . .

"I got up, shut the window, and in coming back remarked that the window was not raised a foot, and that I could not think how he had managed to squeeze through. He arose and said: 'Come and see.' I went with him: he told me to open the window as it was before. I did so: he told me to stand a little distance off; he then went through the open space, head first, quite rapidly, his body being nearly horizontal and apparently rigid. He came in again, feet foremost; and we returned to the other room. It was so dark I could not see clearly how he was supported outside. He did not appear to grasp, or rest upon, the balustrade, but rather to be swung out and in. . . ."

How did Daniel Dunglas Home float in and out of third-floor windows in a horizontal position? Who knows? And who could tell, today, with none of the witnesses available for questioning? There *were* other witnesses, who left written accounts of this strange happening. All we can say here is that it was a dark night. The witnesses agreed on that, at any rate!

Home's levitation and floating performance must have been a remarkable sight, if it really happened as witnesses described it. But *did* it happen? Experts don't agree about it. The late Harry Price wrote* : "Personally, I do not accept this levitation at its face value."

When we try to trace the origins of the Levitation illusion, it's a little difficult to separate the occult from the purely entertaining. And to complicate the search even more, we find legendary accounts of people floating in the air which threaten to enter the record. So let's leave those out completely, after merely mentioning the fact that the Old Testament and the Koran contain descriptions of levitations.

* In his foreword to Miss Jean Burton's biography of Home, *Heyday of a Wizard* (George G. Harrap & Co. Ltd., London, 1948, 10s. 6d.).

Before we consider the conjurer's attempts at levitation, let's get one thing clear: we must distinguish between a levitation and a suspension. A levitation involves the raising into the air of a human being, while a suspension means the placing of a person in an impossible state of disequilibrium, and maintaining him there, sometimes without any visible means of support.

For many centuries travellers in the East have been bringing home tales of people floating in the air. But it's only been within the last hundred and fifty years or so that their tales have attracted much serious attention. Before that, in the days when travel in the East was almost as rare as travel to the moon is today, their narratives were probably dismissed as imaginative lies.

When world travel became more popular, though, people began to compare notes about these travellers' tales. And they found that the accounts tallied sufficiently to justify at least consideration, if not credibility. Furthermore, people in Britain had the chance of seeing levitations performed in their own country. A magician using the name of Ching Lau Lauro, in 1830, was advertising his performance as including "Feats of Strength, in the Character of a Chinese Buffo—Gymnastic Exercises—Concluding his Wonderful Entertainments by Sitting in the Air upon Nothing ! ! ! At the Same Time playing with the GOLDEN BALLS, &c."

Ching Lau Lauro had no doubt based his illusion upon the performance of a Brahmin conjurer who earned some fame in Madras a few years earlier by a curious feat of balancing. This magician carried around with him a short plank, which, by adding four legs, he formed into an oblong stool. In a brass socket on the surface of the stool he used to place upright a hollow bamboo pole, terminating in a V-shaped fork, covered with leather.

Before his performance he would have a blanket held up in front of himself and his apparatus. When the blanket was removed, the audience would see the old Brahmin sitting in he air, four feet from the ground, with the outer edge of one hand touching the fork at the top of the bamboo pole. In the same hand he held a string of beads, which he would thoughtfully count while he held the other hand and arm in an erect posture.

Thomas Frost, in his book, *The Lives of the Conjurors*, written in 1875, reported that when the performance was over, "The blanket was then held up before him, and the spectators heard a gurgling noise, like that occasioned by wind escaping from a bladder or tube, and when the screen was withdrawn, he was again standing on the floor or ground."

History does not relate whether the gurgling noise was caused by the conjurer's apparatus, or whether it was covered by the more simple explanation that the old Brahmin was prone to flatulence. And that's not such a facetious explanation as you might imagine. When the Brahmin died in 1830, he imparted the secret of his trick to nobody, says Frost. The trick was effected, according to "a knowing native," by "holding the breath, clearing the tubular organs, and a peculiar mode of respiration."

There's an idea there for some modern magician to work on. Hold your breath, clear the tubular organs, and adopt a peculiar mode of respiration.

Well—how do you know it won't work unless you try it?

When the gurgling old gentleman died in 1830, and whether he disclosed his secret or not, it wasn't long before another floating magician was sitting about in the air in Madras. That was Sheshal, the Brahmin of the Air. By 1832, people began to suspect that Sheshal had discovered another method of sitting in mid-air. Instead of the breath-holding routine, Sheshal, it was whispered, was connected to the vertical bamboo pole by a steel rod passing up his sleeve and down his back, forming a circular seat.

"The conjecture," says Frost, "was probably not very far from the truth."

But I still think that "tubular organs" explanation was the more exotic.

Whatever Ching Lau Lauro thought about it when he Sat in the Air upon Nothing ! ! ! he did take steps to see that *his* audiences didn't discover his secret. Where the view from the gallery of the theatre would have been too revealing, he closed the gallery to the audience. That suggests, Houdini used to say, that he was supported by an iron bar projecting through the backcloth of the stage.

It took a showman to present a suspension (we've not yet reached levitations) that really made people talk. In 1847, Robert-Houdin, the scholarly French magician, offered the illusion against a background of scientific discovery. It was in that year that the anæsthetic properties of ether were beginning to be used in surgery, and Robert-Houdin at once saw the possibility of what today's showmen would call a tie-up.

"The Ethereal Suspension" was his bill matter, and the title itself was so intriguing that other magicians soon copied it, with slight variations. Compars Herrmann, founder of a great conjuring family, used the same title for the trick. John Henry Anderson, "The Wizard of the North," called it "Chloriforeene Suspension." A German magician, Herr Alexander, whose real name was Heimburger, performed the trick in America, and claimed that he had invented it.

But it was Robert-Houdin's version that set people talking— and guessing. "Suspension in equilibrium by atmospheric air, through the action of concentrated ether" was the programme description of the trick, in which Robert-Houdin's six-year-old son, Eugene Robert, was the subject operated upon.

According to the illustrations of the trick used on Robert-Houdin's posters, the illusion was a double impossibility. They show a plank, one end supported on a trestle, the other end in mid-air. On the *unsupported* end of the plank is a four-legged stool, with a walking cane balanced upright upon it. And at the top of the cane, resting upon its handle by one bent elbow, and reclining in a graceful horizontal position, is little Eugene Robert. His eyes are closed, and his head is supported on his hand as though he is asleep. Beneath him, on the plank, is a bottle, presumably containing ether, from which fumes are wreathing upward.

How, you might ask, did the lad get into such a curious position? Robert-Houdin is reticent, in his *Memoirs*, about the routine, but it appears that the scene opened with the plank resting on two trestles. Three stools were then placed on the plank in a row. The boy stood on the centre stool, and rested his elbows on canes balanced on the side stools. The magician then removed the stool on which his son was standing, leaving the boy supported merely by his elbows. The left-hand stool and cane were then taken away, so that Eugene Robert rested in mid-air supported by his right elbow on the right-hand cane. Robert-Houdin then lifted the boy's body to a horizontal position, and as a climax, removed the trestle which supported the right-hand end of the plank. Thus, not only was the boy reposing horizontally in the air, resting on one elbow, but the plank supporting everything remained horizontal too, despite the fact that it was carrying the weight of the boy and the stool and the cane.

At the early stages of the trick, there was the business with the ether bottle—a master-stroke of a master showman. It brought angry letters from spectators, and the newspapers became a battle-ground for those who protested against "the unnatural father who sacrificed the health of his poor child to the pleasures of the public." Robert-Houdin was threatened with "the terrors of the law" if he did not give up his "inhuman performance."

The trick also brought him a Royal Command performance before the Belgian Royal family. Robert-Houdin was nearly a century ahead of his time in seizing opportunities for publicity. I have little doubt as to who started the series of indignant letters that appeared in the Press.

This fine Suspension illusion was an ingenious example of the use of concealed mechanism. The boy wore an elaborate harness, terminating in a steel bar running down his upper arm and fitting on to the walking cane at the elbow. The arm piece was pivoted at the armpit and a ratchet and pawl on the pivot enabled it to be locked in any desired position. So the boy could balance upright or horizontally as easily as he could have supported himself vertically on his elbows on the parallel bars, or horizontally on his bed.

Magicians of the time had little difficulty in solving the secret of the illusion, and many of them copied it faithfully, even to the extent of almost identical imitations of title and poster illustrations.

It was a magnificent illusion, but compared with the Suspension and Levitation illusions of today it was ungainly and improbable. Illusionist Robert Harbin, who is probably today's most cunning inventor of baffling illusions, has a far better effect to offer. Harbin will suspend *a member of the audience* in a horizontal position, against all the laws of gravity, *anywhere*, provided he has room for the two chairs and plank he uses. No special stage fittings, no rehearsed assistant, no mechanism—just a miracle!

Robert-Houdin's Suspension went the rounds for the best part of twenty years without any significant change until The Fakir of Oolu got to work on it. This exotically-named gentleman also performed under the name of Professor Sylvester. His improvement on Robert-Houdin's Suspension was breath-taking, both in effect and direct simplicity.

Having got his lady assistant into a vertical position, suspended on one elbow, he gave her a spin and she twirled round slowly— still lying horizontally in mid-air. But even more mystifying was the climax, when the Professor took away her sole means of support, the vertical rod under her right arm.

My library contains no explanation of this move, but if I were asked to suggest a solution to the problem, I'd say that the support taken away was a shell, shaped like a bamboo pole. When it was removed, it would leave behind an iron upright covered with material to match the backcloth, and which would not be seen because of this camouflage principle. That's only one way the trick could be done as Sylvester did it. There are others, but that seems to me to be the simplest and most logical.

The spinning effect could be brought about by adaptation of the harness worn by the subject. The pivot at the arm would be locked so that she would remain rigidly horizontal, but a simple form of plate-clutch, which could be freed or locked, would enable the magician to turn her body on a horizontal axis.

Some people will never leave a good thing well alone, and one such was Dr. Lynn, a noted Victorian magician. Lynn used to show the Suspension illusion, but his "improvement" consisted of the addition of a second subject. If a magician can make one person remain suspended in mid-air, it's logical to suppose he can do the same thing with two people. That, apparently, was the opinion of the spectators, who would have been just as mystified by a single victim defying the law of gravity.

Up to now, magicians had been *suspending* various ladies and gentlemen of their companies in mid-air. But in 1867 John Nevil Maskelyne brought the illusion up to date as we know it today, and *levitated* his subject. Using his wife as his assistant when his show opened at the Crystal Palace, J. N. made her rise into the air before the eyes of the audience.

Mrs. Maskelyne was "hypnotised" and lowered slowly into a great stone sarcophagus, from which she gracefully floated upward at the command of the magician, later sinking back into the coffin to be revived by mesmeric passes.

The "coffin" concealed the business end of the mechanism that produced the illusion—a flat board connected to an iron arm passing through the backcloth. This arm was raised by a winch backstage. It was necessary for Maskelyne's Levitation to be produced well up-stage, but since that time alternative methods of raising the "levitee" have made it possible to bring the coffin, couch, or other form of support, nearer to the footlights.

This illusion, with modifications, was exhibited at Maskelyne's for many years, until in 1894 J. N.'s son Nevil added a most convincing touch to it. In a playlet, "Modern Witchery," in which J. N. caused a person to float in the air, the hoop was introduced. This was a large band of flexible steel, and was passed over the levitated assistant from end to end twice—once in each direction. That *proved* there were no hidden connections or supports!

And so it should have proved the fact, on paper. But there's a way of operating the hoop so that although it definitely and positively passes once each way over the floating person, *it never touches the hidden support*. The support in this case is cranked, instead of projecting straight through the backcloth. The hoop passes along one arm of the crank until it can go no farther. It is then turned so that it rotates right round the person, and the side of the hoop which is then innermost is passed along the other arm of the crank and falls free at the other side. This principle is next to impossible to describe in words. Only a diagram can demonstrate it.

I've always thought that this development is typical of the ingenuity of magical invention. As far as I know, such a procedure as passing a hoop along the curves of a crank had never been used for any purpose before. And along comes a magician and *invents* it. You can understand a person saying to himself: "A piston moving along a cylinder will compress a gas at the end of the cylinder." That's a logical development of existing thought. But you just cannot follow the workings of a mind that devises something which can't be explained in words!

In America, the Maskelyne Levitation was staged by Harry Kellar, who entitled it "The Levitation of Princess Karnac." Later, the illusion passed to Howard Thurston, who brought it back to England when he toured this country. Backstage gossip to this day accuses Kellar of having appropriated the illusion without Maskelyne's permission. But as Kellar was also presenting an automaton called Psycho, which was the twin of Maskelyne's Psycho, it seems far more likely that some arrangement had been made between the two illusionists. It's hard to believe that Maskelyne would have allowed Kellar to purloin two of his illusions without action, for J. N. Maskelyne was by nature pugnacious and litigacious when his honour or credit was called in question. There's a legend that Kellar came to London and offered to buy the Levitation illusion from Maskelyne, and met with a refusal to sell. Accordingly, the story continues, he hired Paul Valadon, a magician then working with Maskelyne, and nominated him as Kellar's successor. Paul Valadon is supposed to have taken with him to America the blue-prints of the Levitation illusion and handed them to Kellar.

During the years that John Nevil Maskelyne showed his Levitation illusion, he made an important alteration in the method of lifting the assistant. Instead of using a backstage winch to raise a cranked arm projecting through the backcloth, he decided to hoist the cradle, bearing the assistant, from the flies, by means of fine wires. This called into play the use of an intricate system of weights and counter-balancing weights. Its advantages included the fact that no longer was the illusion anchored to the back of the stage, but that it could be brought well downstage.

It had one overpowering disadvantage, though. Unless the lighting and background were exactly right, the wires could be seen from certain angles in the audience. Also, if the stage-hands weren't trained to the split second, the wires had a disconcerting habit of twanging like a choir of harps.

As I mentioned in another chapter, it was Servais Le Roy who made another alteration to the Levitation illusion. Under the name of "Asrah," it was seen all over the world, and is still seen today. The girl is "hypnotised" in the usual manner, and is lowered on to a decorative couch. Covered with a silken cloth, she is seen to rise in the traditional manner, and to float about gently beneath the cloth. Then, at a command from the magician, the cloth suddenly falls, and the girl is gone. This is a dramatic presentation, and when properly performed creates the perfect illusion that the girl has actually vanished into thin air before the eyes of the audience.

The girl, in this illusion, subsides rapidly into the top of the couch at the moment the cloth is flung over her. A framework made of fine jointed wires holds the outline of the girl as it lies on the couch. The framework is either sewn into the cloth, or is made of such fine construction that it simply falls loose when the cloth falls. In this latter instance, the backcloth must be patterned so as to blend with the fine wire shape as it falls.

And how does the cloth, with its framework, get into mid-air? The answer is just the one you'd expect—it's pulled up on strings. A fine thread at each end is sufficient and a quick release hook lets the cloth fall at the right moment.

There's one important thing you should remember: it's not the secret mechanism that's responsible for the success of a good illusion—it's the presentation of the effect. As magicians so often say: It's not what you do, but the way that you do it. And to prove this, I invite you to go and watch the next illusionist who comes your way performing the Levitation illusion. You've read in this chapter of some of the methods used to make a person apparently float in the air. Now go and see it done—and guess *how* it's done!

If you have the good fortune to see Robert Harbin perform his Levitation—not the Suspension with two chairs and a plank—you'll be completely and utterly baffled. He works it in the centre of the stage well away from the backcloth or the wings. There are, you'll swear, no threads, wires, ropes or iron bars. But the lady—from the audience, mark you!—rises and floats. It's a stage illusion, granted. But it's none the less perfect for that.

The same principle I saw applied during the war by a magician touring with an American U.S.O. show in the East. But—and here's the challenge to the wits!—he didn't use a stage, although it was positively a stage illusion depending upon mechanism. He stood on top of an army truck and levitated the girl. I just didn't believe it—until I spoke to the driver of the truck, who plaintively revealed the secret.

There's a Suspension illusion in which the magician wears a strong harness round the shoulders, terminating in a concealed hook at his waist. His assistant, too, wears a harness which engages with the hook on the magician's belt. The girl can be *suspended* there without any need for the secret mechanisms of a well-equipped stage. But she won't rise and fall, as did the girl levitated by the American magican with the truck.

How's it done? Oh, it's done easily enough. But it's such a clever secret that I think it ought to remain a secret—don't you?

And if you *do* succeed in finding how it's done, then I refer you to a further challenge to the wits. This is presented, on rare occasions when he feels like it, by Bobby Voltaire. The last time I heard of his doing it was a few years ago when he performed it on a seaside beach. It's not a levitation, but a suspension, and what makes it so absolutely impossible is the fact that Bobby and his girl assistant wear bathing costumes!

Some philosopher once discovered that what goes up must come down. But magicians know differently, as you'll agree when you see your next Levitation illusion.

Chapter Eight

SAWING A WOMAN IN HALF

You might think that a sensational spectacle like Sawing a
Woman in Half had a long and honourable history. It hasn't.
It was first performed in London in 1921. Since then, at least
four stage versions and two excellent cabaret versions have
been developed. Every illusionist of note has presented Sawing
a Woman in Half, and although the principles they use have
been exposed many times, the audiences are still thrilled and
mystified.

Percy Tibbles, an English magician working under the name
of P. T. Selbit, was the originator of the trick, and his version
still remains one of the most baffling of all. In Selbit's original
illusion, a girl is placed in a long wooden box which just fits her
height. In each side of the box are two one-inch holes, one pair
at shoulder level and the others near her ankles. The girl raises
her hands to her shoulders, and a rope is passed through each of
the upper holes and is attached to her wrists. The ends of the
rope are held by spectators. Two more ropes are tied round her
ankles, and the ends of these are again held by members of the
audience. Another rope goes round her neck.

The girl is thus securely fixed in the box, so that she cannot
move her head, her hands, or her feet.

The box is laid upon four trestles, and the lid is placed on it.
The magician and one of his assistants take a two-handled saw,
and cut right through the box—and, presumably, the girl!
Panels of wood are placed vertically over the cut ends of the
box, and the two halves of the box are drawn apart.

When they are placed together again, and the vertical panels
are withdrawn, the lid is opened, and there the girl is seen, still
secured by the ropes at her neck, wrists and ankles. She is cut
free of the ropes, and emerges from the box quite unharmed.

The box, the saw, the trestles and the ropes are all free from trickery, and can be examined before and afterwards.

Where, then, is the trick?

The girl carries the secret of it in her right hand, in the form of a sharp scrap of razor blade. Once the lid's placed on the box, she pulls enough of the right-hand rope in to enable her to cut the knots at her left wrist. The razor blade is then taken in her left hand and she cuts the rope round her right wrist and round her neck. The box is deep enough to enable her to crouch in one end of it, and so when the saw passes through the sides of the box she is well out of its path. The vertical panels are slid between the two cut portions of the box so that nobody can see the girl huddled in one end of it. When the panels are removed, and the halves of the box placed together, she resumes her former position, places her wrists against the ends of the cut ropes, and draws the other piece of rope round her neck again. The magician opens the box, cuts the *already cut* ropes, and there she is, unharmed!

That is the bare outline of the illusion. Some of the finer details include the method of tying the ropes round her wrists and neck so that a large knot inside the box prevents the cut ropes being pulled out of their holes. The timing of the whole procedure must be carefully watched, so that the right wrist rope is slackened for a second to allow the girl to make the first cut, and—most important!—to give her time to get into the end of the box.

It was simple of execution and dramatic in presentation, and was probably the finest illusion of the century when Selbit first staged it in London. It must have been good, because within weeks other magicians had imitated the effect both here and in America!

The way in which Sawing a Woman in Half was copied was not too ethical, to say the least. Horace Goldin, the famous American illusionist (who was actually of Russian-Polish extraction), heard about Selbit's impressive spectacle. Goldin used to say: "Give me an effect, and I'll find a method of producing it." This was one time when he lived up to his word. Without having seen the illusion, he and his associates worked out a method of performing it—a method which was completely different from that used by Selbit.

He built the apparatus for his method, and at once started to protect himself against imitators. In July, 1921, a few weeks after Selbit's audience had been startled by the first showing of Sawing a Woman in Half, Goldin was exhibiting his effect. He had associates presenting it in different cities, so that before long the market was, you might say, flooded with Women being Sawn in Halves. But even so, Goldin wasn't content. He arranged for copyists to be served with injunctions forbidding them to perform the illusion. One writer claims that Goldin made a net profit of $40,000 from the combine, of which he spent $14,000 on injunctions and litigation.

The result was that Selbit himself, the inventor and first performer of the illusion, was prevented from showing it in America. As Goldin's presentation and method were both different from Selbit's, though, Goldin could, and did, bring his version to England. Goldin performed the Sawing illusion for years all over the world, and today the general impression seems to be that he invented the illusion. He didn't. He invented *his way of performing it*.

Later, after Goldin died, many other magicians performed the illusion, with variations. And it was some of the variations which finally put the public on the scent of the method used. That's often the case with magic. A perfectly good, mystifying, entertaining trick is originated, and before you can say "Hey, Presto!" it's been copied and "improved." In the end, some of the "improved" versions have become so fantastic that the original trick is lost sight of.

Goldin's version of Sawing a Woman in Half was ingenious and baffling as he designed it. A large box was laid upon a low table. The top and the front of the box were hinged, so that it could be seen to be empty—which it was. A girl was placed in the box, with her head projecting from one end and her feet from the other. The whole affair, box, table and all, was turned slowly round so that the audience could see it from all angles. The box was now sawn in half down the middle of the long side. Panels were placed at the division, and the box was drawn apart, while the girl's head and feet were still seen to be projecting. The eighteen-inch space in the middle showed that the head and the feet were quite separated.

But that was because *they belonged to different girls.*

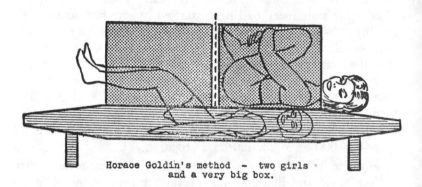

Horace Goldin's method - two girls
and a very big box.

SAWING A WOMAN IN HALF

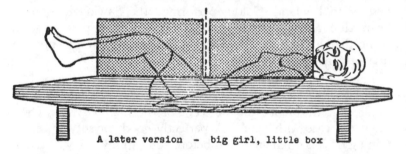

A later version - big girl, little box

Yes, there was a second girl. She was hidden in the top of the low table. When the apparatus was turned round slowly, the first girl drew her feet inside the box and the second girl thrust hers out through the same holes. The bottom of the box was provided with a trap to enable the second girl to do this, and the necessary cover for the exchange of feet was provided by the turning round of the box. The exchange was made when the "feet" end of the box was turned away from the audience.

The box was big enough—that always seemed the weak point to me—to allow the first girl to draw up her legs and contain herself in the upper end of the box. So when the saw went through the box, it touched neither girl.

At the end of the illusion, the table and box were turned round again, and the first girl put her feet through the holes at the other end, as soon as the second girl had drawn hers in.

Some illusionists who performed this effect used to have the first girl wriggle her feet so that one of her shoes fell off. Then, when the box and table had been turned round, and the second girl's feet would be showing, it would be noticed that there was a shoe missing from one foot. It would be replaced casually, but with enough display to make sure the audience saw and noted the fact. The second girl, of course, was wearing only one shoe from the start. It meant that both girls had to have the same size feet. It also meant that the first girl had to remember which shoe to shake off. I once saw that irascible magician, Dante, puzzled because the girl had lost the wrong shoe. After a thoughtful pause, he clapped a left shoe on the second girl's right foot. There was much squirming of the foot and a muffled complaint seemed to come from inside the box.

It was Dante, too, who added one of the needless "improvements" to the Sawing illusion. Normally, the table top was so made that its extra thickness would not be noticed, but Dante actually drew attention to the table top by having large holes in it which permitted the audience to see right through it. When the box was turned, and the exchange of feet was made, a mirror fell into place behind the holes so that the audience could not see through them.

Whereupon, of course, the more intelligent members of the audience asked themselves why the table top should be made so thick at all.

In the various adaptations of Horace Goldin's Sawing method, the table top is deep enough in the middle to contain the second girl. At the edges it is possibly three inches thick, but to secure this bevel, it's necessary to have a table top much longer and wider than would be needed if the girl was *really* sawn in half. Clever craftsmanship in the building and decorating of the table hides the bulge in the middle fairly effectively, but it can't shorten the length and make the width seem reasonable.

A later method, using a faked table but only one girl, soon followed Goldin's first version. In this variation, which really is an improvement, apart from the thick table top, the box is shorter than the girl, so that she has to bend her body to get in. Her head projects at one end, and her feet at the other, but when the two halves of the box are drawn apart, after the sawing, they can't be moved far. In this method, the middle of the girl's body sinks into the table top, and a protective strip of steel is lowered over her to prevent the saw blade accidentally touching her.

Needless to say, the box has trap doors in the bottom to enable the girl to lower her hips into the table top.

Goldin staged a further variation at the London Palladium in July, 1931, when he *sawed a girl in half without using a box.* This was truly dramatic, and was made even more horrifying by the use of a circular saw, descending slowly on to the girl and ripping through her body. Or so it seemed. Actually, the girl was safe and sound inside the table top again, and what the saw cut through was merely a shell that fitted round her body and was left on the table top when her hips dropped into the hollow table.

The indefatigable Goldin, two years after that, in March, 1933, filed suit against an American tobacco company, to restrain the company from revealing an explanation of the Sawing in Half illusion in advertisements for their cigarettes. Goldin claimed that he had conceived the illusion in 1911 and had since patented it, and that the so-called explanation was a violation of his rights. He further claimed that the advertisements had affected his ability to get bookings.

For this alleged violation of rights, Goldin asked for $50,000 damages. The suit lingered on for five years, and in 1938 was dismissed. The Court held that the tobacco company had obtained the information they published by legitimate means, from a book written by Mr. Walter Gibson.

If Goldin conceived the idea for the illusion in 1911, I can't see why he waited ten years to produce it.

Since those brisk days, other illusionists have really improved and dramatised the Sawing in Half illusion. Kalanag carries it out at high speed and with great dramatic effect. Sorcar, the Indian illusionist, performed it with such zest when he brought his show to London, that the audience really thought he *had* sawn the girl in half! Richiardi, a South American magician, makes a most blood-curdling business of it, with blood and guts flying all over the stage. That I would *not* like to see.

I do not propose to explain how these three methods are worked, for the plain reason that I don't know. In any case, the Sawing illusion has travelled so far since those days in 1921, when magicians sued each other so readily, and audiences fainted right, left and centre, that we should allow its present method of performance to remain a secret.

Likewise too good to reveal is the secret of the illusion known as the Portable Sawing in Half. In this version, which can be performed on a ballroom floor in the middle of a surrounding audience, the girl is laid on a plank supported by two chairs. A light framework, to guide the saw, is placed over her middle, and the saw passes right through her. *Does* it pass right through her? Well, it finishes up underneath her, after being passed through the frame from the top. What do *you* think?

And in case you think that a specially trained assistant is used as the victim, let me add that with this method, *any* lady (or any gentleman, too, for that matter) can be deftly bisected and restored. This was the method used by Robert Harbin when he sawed through Brian Johnstone in a BBC broadcast a few years ago. Harbin also used it at the Magic Circle Clubroom when the Duke of Edinburgh was a guest of the Circle. The victim in this case was the Duke's aide. "You'll feel twice the man you were, after this!" quipped Harbin, as he and the Duke busily sawed through the officer.

If Selbit were alive now, I'm sure he'd chuckle with sheer delight to see the progress his Sawing illusion had made over the years. When he planned his original illusion, he must have realised that the ideal way to do it would be without the box or other bulky apparatus, in the middle of the floor with the audience all round, and using a person from the audience as the subject.

I believe Selbit invented Sawing a Woman in Half after reading the account of a similar performance which, many authorities believe, never took place. That was the spectacular performance of Torrini, or the Count de Grisy as he was alternatively called, narrated to Robert-Houdin early in the last century. Students of magical history now doubt whether there ever was a Torrini or a Count de Grisy. They believe that Robert-

Houdin invented him and introduced a fictitious history of him into *The Memoirs of Robert-Houdin* merely for dramatic effect.

Read this extract from Robert-Houdin's *Memoirs,* and see how closely it tallies with a present-day performance of the box version of the Sawing in Half. The narrator is the legendary Torrini, and he says to Robert-Houdin : —

"At my summons, two slaves brought in a long and narrow chest, and a trestle for sawing wood. Antonio seemed to be terribly alarmed, but I coldly ordered the slaves to seize him, place him in the chest, the cover of which was immediately nailed down, and lay it across the trestle. Then, taking up a saw, I prepared to cut the chest asunder. . . . The chest was at last divided into two parts; I raised them so that each represented a pedestal; I then placed them side by side and covered them with an enormous wicker cone. . . . Suddenly, the deep silence was interrupted by two voices performing an exquisite duet beneath the black cloth. . . . Two pages, exactly alike, appeared on the pedestals. . . ."

Torrini, according to Robert-Houdin's story, had climaxed the effect by producing two people, instead of following today's fashion and restoring the two halves to one whole person.

If Selbit designed his illusion from this idea, he certainly presented it to greater advantage by making use of a single person, and securing her in the box beforehand.

It's been suggested from time to time that the Sawing in Half Illusion owes its invention to the ancient Indian Basket Trick. My personal view is that it descends direct from the pages of Robert-Houdin's *Memoirs.*

The Indian Basket Trick is indeed ancient. Ibn Batuta and other old travellers report having seen it in one form or another, and we needn't doubt their word. The Indian Basket Trick is today often seen in sideshows, and sometimes in the theatre. There isn't a lot of mystery about it. A boy or a girl is placed in a large flat basket beneath a net or a sheet. The magician sticks knives or swords through the basket, dances about inside it, and generally conducts himself to prove that the boy or girl has vanished. The trick is more hair-raising to read about than to see, as the following comment from the London *Daily News* for April 18th, 1865, goes to prove : —

"Colonel Stodare has introduced one illusion which, though often heard of, has, we believe, never before been seen in this country—the famous Indian Basket Trick. A huge hamper is placed upon a stand, so as to leave a perfectly clear space between the bottom and the floor. A young lady is then shut up in this basket, and Colonel Stodare makes repeated passes through the wickerwork with a sword. The audience are horrified while this is going on by hearing piercing screams, and by seeing the blade come out dripping with blood; but when the cries have at length ceased, and a horrible murder has (notwithstanding Horace's caution) been to all appearances committed in the presence of the assembly, the basket is found to be empty, and the victim is brought back into the room safe and sound. This part of his performance is unquestionably one of the most startling feats ever exhibited."

That was a report of Stodare's first showing of the Basket Trick at London's Egyptian Hall in Piccadilly.

I think you might care to hear some of the patter used in this trick. Robert-Houdin cites it in his *Secrets of Stage Conjuring,* although his translator, Professor Hoffmann, waxes a little sniffy at Robert-Houdin for criticising the trick at all. It was hardly likely, said Professor Hoffmann in his restrained way, that Robert-Houdin ever saw Stodare perform the trick.

The patter, then:

(*The Colonel comes forward, followed by a handsome boy, wearing with native grace the traditional costume of an Indian prince. . . .*)

The Colonel: What do I behold? A descendant of that hated race which has shed so much English blood!

The Prince (*gently*): Nay, I am only a child.

The Colonel: That will not prevent me from putting you to death!

The Prince: Spare me! Spare me!

The Colonel: I cannot spare you; you must die!

(*The boy seeks to escape, but in vain. The Colonel seizes him, thusts him into the basket, draws his sword, and, after proving its sharpness by thrusting its point deep into the flooring of the stage, makes repeated lunges at the basket. At every thrust, the child utters a scream of agony. The sword is withdrawn each*

*time, dripping with the blood of the victim. The shrieks grow
weaker and weaker, and after a few moments all is silence.*)

The Spectators: Enough! Enough! (*Indescribable horror.
Ladies hide their faces with their fans and beg for mercy.*)

Well!

That's how Robert-Houdin described it, anyway. It's all there
in the book.

So much for the Sword Basket—and enough, too!

Another startling illusion which may have inspired Selbit,
though I doubt it, is the famous Sword Cabinet. In this, a girl
is placed in a vertical cabinet and secured therein, and swords
are pushed through from all directions. Sounds simple enough,
doesn't it? So it would be, if we didn't consider the girl. In
some versions of the Sword Cabinet, the girl is enclosed by fold-
ing mirrors when the doors are opened, so that a mass of swords
is seen, but no girl. In others, the doors are only opened at the
beginning, when the girl gets in, and at the end, when she steps
out.

Gil Leaney, the London magician, presents what I think is
the most mystifying version of the Sword Cabinet. His girl
assistant, Frankie, is firmly secured in the cabinet, the doors are
shut, and the swords are thrust through the walls and door.
There is apparently no space left for Frankie to occupy, that
isn't already occupied by sword blades.

But just when you're beginning to think the whole thing's
impossible, Leaney pushes a twelve-inch wide steel blade through
the top half of the cabinet. Another blade goes through the lower
half. And still another is thrust, horizontally, through the
middle.

I've stood backstage with expert illusionists and heard them
say, as the last blade goes through: "It just isn't possible! There
is nowhere—but nowhere—for Frankie to put herself!"

But every time so far, Frankie has survived.

Incidentally, I imagine that Frankie Lovett is the most sawn-
in-half, levitated-in-the-air, sword-menaced, envanished, and be-
witched-generally girl in London.

Perhaps she ought to have written this chapter. She could
really tell what it feels like to be sawn in half. Which is more
than I can say about myself.

Chapter Nine

THE LEGEND OF HOUDINI

STOP A DOZEN people and ask them each to name a magician. Ten of them will name Houdini, you may be sure.

That's odd, you know, because you'd have to be getting on for fifty years old to be able to say you saw Houdini perform. It's more than thirty years since Houdini died, and yet his name is among the first associated with magic by young people whose parents may not even have met when Houdini died.

Houdini is a legend today, even as he was in his own lifetime.

But what *do* people know about him, after these thirty years and more?

Ask a few. You'll get some amazing answers.

Some will tell you, in all seriousness, that Harry Houdini was able to dematerialise himself in order to escape from the restraints that were put upon him during his performances. Others will say that he was in league with the devil—witchcraft, mind you, in the Twentieth Century! And then you'll meet people who can tell you all about him—or so they imagine. "Yes, I know about Houdini," they'll say. "I saw the film about him."

So they may have done. But it was a garbled story the film told.

And you? What do you know about Houdini? It's a fair bet that you could tell us plenty about the Handcuff King. Why, you may even have seen that amazing condensed story of his life that was screened on British Broadcasting Corporation's television some time ago. And that, probably, was the oddest piece of legend ever perpetrated. If only Houdini could have lived to see the B.B.C.'s idea of his Vanishing Elephant illusion!

Yes, there are more Houdini legends than you could count. And many of them, without doubt, were either fostered or originated by Houdini himself.

111

But if you want to be accurate when next you talk about Houdini, you can say that he was born on April 6th, 1874, at Appleton, Wisconsin, U.S.A. His father was a Jewish rabbi named Mayer Samuel Weiss, and Houdini's given name was Ehrich. He died on October 31st, 1926, in Detroit.

Young Ehrich Weiss started his theatrical career when he was nine years old. Somehow, he persuaded the proprietor of a circus visiting his home town to allow him to perform a few turns on the trapeze. The engagement was a short one, for Mrs. Weiss had other plans for her Ehrich. She walked straight into the tent of circus chief Jack Hoffler, and five minutes later walked out again—with Ehrich clutched firmly by his resined little paw.

From time to time, Ehrich Weiss got himself other jobs in travelling circuses, but his mother and father resolutely set themselves against this sort of work. A steady job, and none of this theatrical nonsense, was what they planned for Ehrich. And so they apprenticed him to a locksmith. You'll often hear tales of young Weiss's skill while he worked as a locksmith, but the fact is that he *hated* the job. As soon as he could (in his own words), he "made a bolt for the door and never again entered the locksmith's shop."

This time, though, he was a few years older, and managed to persuade his parents that he was old enough to know his own mind. Again, he got himself a job with a circus, where he worked as clown, ventriloquist—and conjurer.

Henry Ridgely Evans, the great historian of the magic arts, tells the tale of Houdini's first great escape—still, though, under the name of Ehrich Weiss.

"He made a speciality of the rope-tying business and performed occasionally with handcuffs, but without sensational results," writes Evans in *The Old and The New Magic*. "Finally the circus landed in Rhode Island, and opened up in a town where Sunday performances were forbidden by law, but were greatly desired by a large section of the population. As the fine was light, the proprietor ran the risk, and gave a show on the Sabbath. A summons followed, and each member of the troupe was fined. As Houdini epigrammatically put it: 'The manager couldn't find the fine, so we all found ourselves in confinement.'

"Houdini was locked up in a cell with a number of side-show freaks, the fat lady, the living skeleton, and the German giant. The fat lady was too wide for the compartment, the giant too long. With tears in their eyes they implored Houdini to pick the lock and let them out. Finally, the young conjurer consented, and dexterously picked the lock, whereupon he and his companions marched out of the jail in triumph, and paraded down the main street of the town in Indian file, to the great amusement of the populace. Houdini was rearrested on the charge of jail-breaking, but the judge let him off with a reprimand. This event decided his career. He became a Handcuff King."

Well—it could have happened, I suppose. But it sounds far more like one of Houdini's own stories than a factual report.

It was a book that changed Ehrich Weiss into Harry Houdini, a book written fifteen years before the boy was born. The author was Robert-Houdin, one of the greatest magicians of all time. Young Weiss was so fascinated by Robert-Houdin's *Memoires*, that he adopted the stage name of Houdini, adding the first name, Harry, for the sake of alliteration. Later, Houdini suffered a change of views about his former idol, and went to enormous trouble to write a long, bitter attack on Robert-Houdin. This tirade he called *The Unmasking of Robert-Houdin,* and it earned him little credit. It was a long, well-produced and lavishly illustrated book. Read it, and you will get the impression that Robert-Houdin was no more than a mediocre mountebank who stole other magicians' secrets and presented them as his own. But don't leave it at that. Read Robert-Houdin's *Memoires* as well, and then go on to read what other students of the theatre have to say about Robert-Houdin. Especially, read Mons. Maurice Sardina's answer to Houdini, *Les Erreurs de Harry Houdini** and *then* form your opinion of Houdini as a reliable critic. In his later years, Houdini told the veteran English magician and authority of magical history, Chris Charlton, that he was beginning to regret having written *The Unmasking.*

No wonder. It was a needless, vicious attack on a man who, in his time, was quite as famous and respected a figure as Houdini ever was. More, Robert-Houdin was dead and could

---

* English translation, *Where Houdini Was Wrong,* published by The Magic Wand Publishing Company, London

not reply to it. So is Houdini, now, and so I have no more to say about *The Unmasking of Robert-Houdin.*

It may have been Houdini's personal vanity that contributed to his death. All his life he had been a fine athlete, and the fact was one of the highlights of his publicity campaigns. When he was performing in Montreal, in October, 1926, he discussed physical fitness with a group of students. Suddenly, one of them struck him a blow in the stomach, to test Houdini's claim that he could withstand such a blow. But the magician was not expecting the attack, and was not able to brace his muscles to receive the blow.

A few days later, after moving on to his next engagement in Detroit, he died. He was buried, according to his own wish, in a great bronze coffin he used in one of his illusions.

Today, Houdini lies buried in the Machpelah Cemetery, Cypress Hills, Long Island. For thirty years the bronze casket has rested in the quiet cemetery, where he was buried with Masonic honours.

Thirty years. And yet today Houdini's name is as well known as it was in his heyday. Houdini the aggressive assailant of Robert-Houdin is forgotten. Houdini the legend lives on.

He could get out of anything, people say to this day. Nothing could hold Houdini, they declare. He baffled the police of the world. Lock him, naked, in a police cell, and the minute your back was turned, he'd be out, they'll tell you.

How true are these legends?

Oh, they're true enough. Houdini did all these things. And more. Much more. What a showman the man was!

Yes, it really *did* seem as though Houdini could get out of anything.

Houdini *made* it seem that way. The more difficult, the more complicated and dangerous an escape was, the more he revelled in it—and the more often his name was blazoned across the world's headlines. Publicity was his life blood. And he challenged death many times to achieve that publicity.

Mind you, Houdini was no fool. He would consider carefully whether an escape was within his powers before even planning it. And when he knew he could do it, he would start people talking about it *before he did it.* That way, he created suspense.

What use to Houdini would a private escape be, an escape with nobody to marvel at it?

It wasn't by chance that members of his audience brought their own handcuffs and restraints to the theatre, to challenge The Handcuff King. They'd heard, perhaps, that this would be a stiff test for Houdini. Maybe he wouldn't be able to get out of somebody else's handcuffs. Maybe Houdini's own apparatus was faked. Maybe . . .

Maybe Houdini started those rumours!

You can take it as certain that if, for example, ordinary regulation police handcuffs were impossible to escape from, Houdini would have directed the public's attention to some other form of restraint. As it was, he would foster the rumour that regulation handcuffs really *were* a tough proposition. And strait-jackets! Why, it was next to impossible to get out of a regulation strait-jacket!

So there arose the spectacle—never beheld since—of respectable citizens lining up at the box office with jingling handcuffs in their pockets, or a bulky parcel containing a strait-jacket under their arms.

Are regulation handcuffs hard to escape from? The answer is a plain and definite "No!"—especially if you have access to a key. For, you see, regulation handcuffs have regulation keys, and such keys are small, easily concealed objects. Even if you don't have a key, you can spring the lock of most handcuffs by striking them smartly on a hard surface. It may take you a long time to get the knack of it, but once you have it, you can open any pair of that make of handcuffs in that way. Houdini, of course, had worked for many years on an exhaustive study of the world's handcuffs, and could recognise at a glance the treatment needed to open almost any pair brought to him.

He and his agents scoured the patents offices of the world. His stock of keys numbered hundreds, and he made no secret of the fact, when talking to magicians, that no handcuff locked and opened by a key could baffle him. There were handcuffs, though, which he would not tackle. One favourite ruse of troublesome challengers was to drop a steel ball-bearing into the lock of a pair of spring handcuffs. This meant that the cuffs could be sprung on and locked, but that no key could reach the screw thread inside, and that the lock was immovably wedged once it was closed. Such handcuffs he would throw scornfully back to the challenger, with a scathing denunciation of people who didn't play fair.

It was Houdini's practice, from a very early date in his career, to demand that a challenge pair of handcuffs, or indeed any lock offered to him as a test, should be locked and opened in front of himself and the audience, just to prove that it was possible to open it. A wise precaution! Any conjurer will tell you with horror of the "narks" to be encountered in the magic game!

If a key was needed, then Houdini didn't have far to look to find that key. But he was searched!—you may say. So he may have been. Have *you* ever searched a man? If you can answer "Yes," you'll probably admit that you've exercised some delicacy about it. After all, there are limits . . . .

Houdini knew that most people feel that way, and so he knew just where to hide a key.

For example, let's say that you and a few friends had agreed to act as the committee on the stage, and to search Houdini minutely behind a screen. All right. You had every stitch of clothing off him, and you searched every pocket and every seam of that clothing without finding anything. You searched Houdini physically, not overlooking his thick, bushy hair. Still no key.

But—didn't you forget one simple hiding place? No? You scrapped all delicacy and searched everywhere? You did?

Then what about those two keys he carried under his feet, hidden under the curl of his toes?

Houdini had long, àgile toes which he could use as fingers to a certain extent, and was not difficult for him to grip a key in his toes just as you might grip one in your fist. If you'd made him sit down and hold up his feet so that you could prise his toes open, do you think you'd have found those keys?

You'd have been too late! Another member of the committee, a stranger to you and the others, would have been first to examine his toes, if the subject had been mentioned. And that stranger would have removed the keys, later giving them back to Houdini as he shook hands on leaving.

I mention this as one example of Houdini's deep cunning, and I use the word in the best, most appreciative sense. Houdini pitted his wits against the wits of the world, and won every time —with but very, very few exceptions. Please don't think, though, that Houdini habitually carried keys in his toes. That was just one subterfuge he used, and he used it rarely. I cite it only to show how it is possible to deceive a conscientious stage committee.

Not long ago, I was present when a famous young magician performed what's known as the Blindfold Drive for some news-papermen. He was heavily blindfolded by them, and then challenged to drive a car round the block. To make sure that there was no possibility of the magician's seeing through his bandages, the Pressmen invited a medical specialist to check their blindfolding. The doctor twisted the magician's head this way and that, and if there was the least chink in the bandages, he would have seen it.

He announced that the newspapermen had done a good job in their bandaging. Then the magician was guided into the car, his hand was placed on the ignition key and his foot on the starter. The engine started. His hand was guided to the gear-change lever—and he was OFF! Off, with four scared news-papermen as his passengers, as he drove a tortuous way through London's busy traffic!

Who made it possible for him to perfom this daring feat after strangers—and awkward strangers, at that!—had made it im-possible for him to see?

I'll tell you.

The doctor made the necessary slight arrangement of the blindfold which ensured the success of the illusion. The doctor is a prominent amateur magician.

Now I hope you won't imagine that every magician who per-forms the Blindfold Drive has the help of a confederate. Indeed, it's much easier to perform this spectacular illusion without any help, and there are many ways of doing it. But that's another story!

Houdini never hesitated to use a confederate if the occasion called for it. But the great majority of his tricks and illusions, as well as most of his escapes, needed no such aid. When it came to a challenge from the police, though, a confederate was often the only answer to the problem Houdini had been set. After all, if police searchers (and they know about hiding things in the toes, *and* everywhere else!) had gone over their man thoroughly, there'd be precious little hiding space left for a key. And once locked in a bare, scrubbed cell, there'd be precious little chance of getting out of it, either.

And so the one sure, easy method was to use a confederate. Long before being locked in the cell, Houdini would make the reasonable request that he should see the door locked and unlocked. That meant that he would also see the key, and probably be allowed to handle it. Remember that Houdini had been a locksmith. Handling a key, and perhaps finding the opportunity to take an impression of it in wax or soap, gave all the information he needed to make a duplicate key. This would be entrusted to his secret ally, who would accompany the police searchers and see the cell securely locked. But before he left, he would contrive to pass the key to Houdini, or to leave it somewhere in the cell.

How could a key be passed to Houdini, when all eyes were on him, watching his every movement? One way was to pass it to him in the course of a handshake, while wishing him the best of luck. Sometimes, the confederate slipped the key into a glass of water Houdini had called for, and it slid into the magician's mouth as he drank.

Happily, I can say that I know little about prison cells and the mechanism of their doors and locks. But I do know enough to be aware that many cells nowadays only open from the outside, and have no keyhole inside. Houdini knew it, too. And if you tell me that he ever got out of such a cell by using a key while he was *inside* I'd say it just wasn't possible.

What would a magician do if confronted by such a position? The first thing would be to make little of escaping from such a cell. But if he saw a practicable cell which *could* be broken, then he'd shy away from it in alarm. Oh, no! Not that!

The result would be that his challengers would insist on *that*!

Psychology was the most valuable instrument in Houdini's kit. Skeleton keys, confederates, cleverly faked apparatus—these are useless if you can't handle people. Houdini was an expert psychologist. People in his hands would do as *he* wanted, not as they wanted. He had charm, persuasive, devastating charm which all the films, all the books, and all the television shows about him have never portrayed. It was an intimate, between-you-and-me, friendly, smiling charm which was completely over-powering. But it could turn to icy scorn or blazing anger if he was faced with a tough customer. The charm, though, won over the audience, and they were on his side if he had to turn his anger on a "nark."

That isn't to say that skeleton keys, confederates, and faked apparatus weren't used. They were—extensively.

Think it over. A magician is going to escape, say, from a giant milk churn filled with water.

Where is the milk churn going to be found that will hold a man?

Where else but among a magician's apparatus?

Such props were audience-proof and examination-proof, and you'd never find the secret exit in a month of Sundays. They'd pass the strictest scrutiny every time, and so would be accepted by the examining committee as genuine articles.

But the milk churn, for instance, was as easy to get out of as your car. Two of the rivets near the top could be turned, and the whole inside would slide upwards like a cork out of a bottle. Once out, Houdini would replace the "stopper" while the band played a double-forte march. He would then lock the fake rivets back in place, sit down on the floor of his curtained cabinet, and wait. Suspense was being built up, as the members of the audience looked at their watches, pursed their lips, and shook their heads. Two minutes — three minutes — four minutes — five minutes. How *could* a man stay in a cramped steel milk churn so long, and *under water, too?*

And when at last, the band having played through *Zampa, Under the Double Eagle,* and the *Light Cavalry Overture,* Houdini stepped out, dripping and breathless, what applause there was!

Many of the articles from which Houdini escaped—boxes, trunks, coffins, steel chests—could be opened from the inside only after the lid or door was closed. That meant that no inquisitive member of the audience could ever find the secret catch without

getting inside and being shut in. And Houdini's stage staff would
see to it that the examination never went so far. Any member of
the audience was at liberty, and welcome, to examine the
apparatus minutely. But until he got inside and was locked in,
he would never find the secret of getting out!

You would see Houdini and his staff *helping* the committee
from the audience to examine the apparatus. Obligingly, the lid
of the trunk would be flung open—and an assistant would hold
it open! Have the lid shut? Certainly! And the lid was flung
down with a heavy clang while the earnest inquirers had the box

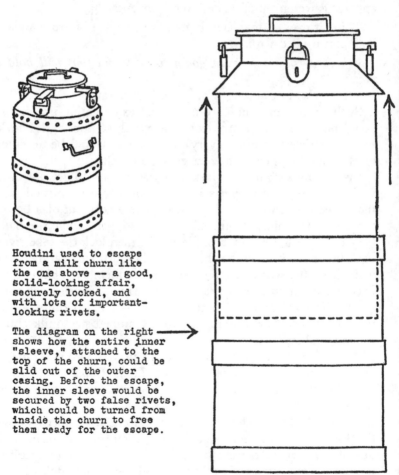

Houdini used to escape
from a milk churn like
the one above -- a good,
solid-looking affair,
securely locked, and
with lots of important-
looking rivets.

The diagram on the right ——→
shows how the entire inner
"sleeve," attached to the
top of the churn, could be
slid out of the outer
casing. Before the escape,
the inner sleeve would be
secured by two false rivets,
which could be turned from
inside the churn to free
them ready for the escape.

turned over. But never—never!—did anyone think of getting inside and having the lid closed on him. Perhaps that's a sweeping statement. Perhaps many people thought of it. But there's no record of anyone *doing* it! No. Houdini, his manager and his staff would see to that.

And remember : the only way to get *out* of the trunk was first to get *in*.

One of the Houdini legends people never tire of retailing is the one about the rubber straps on the strait-jacket. There may be a way of escaping from a strait-jacket that has a rubber strap or two on it. I don't know. But I do know that it's easier to get out of a strait-jacket with hard, rigid straps. Any escapologist will tell you, if you're in his confidence, that any restraint that "gives" is a bad one to get out of. You just can't get any tension on the places where it's needed if the strait-jacket stretches.

So please believe that Houdini really did get out of his strait-jackets by main force and amazing suppleness. A man trained to do it makes light work of such an escape. But he's got to be tough—tough and resilient. His muscles must be able to stretch more than yours and mine. His joints must have that little extra degree of flexibility. And he's got to be able to breathe properly. That means perfectly maintained physical fitness. Without it, nobody could make the first move to get out of a strait-jacket— that first slow, wrenching, powerful leverage of the crooked arm over the head. That done, he simply *must* carry on, if he isn't to dislocate an arm or tear a ligament, for the arms are drawn into an intolerably painful position when one hand's been manœuvred behind the shoulders.

No, there's no trick in escaping from a strait-jacket. It's sheer strength, coupled with the skill and know-how that only comes with long practice.

Ropes and chains are a different thing, though. It's knack— and experience—that gets a magician out of those. Houdini used to say there was only one tie that he couldn't escape from, and that could be made with nine inches of button thread.

If you want to see whether *you* could escape from a thread tie, get a friend to tie you up like this : First, sit on the ground, with your knees drawn up to your chin. Then have a broomstick placed beneath your knees. Pass your arms under the broomstick, and allow your friend to tie your thumbs together in front of your shins. Nine inches of thread is just about long enough to make a good sound job of it.

Now, with practice, you'll find that you can get out of this one. You might be able to stretch your tied hands down over your feet. You may even wriggle the broomstick out of place. Or you might prefer to raise your hands and bite through the thread.

Anyway, having got out of it, don't congratulate yourself too soon. There's worse to come!

Now, lie on your face and bring your feet up behind you. Again, have the broomstick thrust behind the knees. If your friend (and he'd be no friend of mine!) now draws your hands down so that he can tie your thumbs over your ankles, you'll be *really* tied up. That's the one that Houdini dreaded!

But nevertheless, Houdini wasn't the man to be beaten by a bit of thread. Although he might not have been able to escape legitimately, he'd have got out of the thread tie all right. If I were challenged to get out of this one, I'd make sure that a scrap of razor blade was available somewhere. With it, I'd cut the thread between the thumbs, and from that stage it would be an easy step to free each thumb. Then I'd loop a spare piece of thread round the thumbs and finish off the tie with my teeth. At the finish, I'd be standing up, with my thumbs still tied, apparently as they were at the beginning.

One of Houdini's most spectacular escapes was from a giant-sized paper bag, sealed with sealing wax along the top edge after he'd been placed inside. After the escape, the seals would be intact, and there would be no trace of the bag's having been tampered with in any way. This truly mystifying illusion is so simple to prepare and to execute that I am always amazed nobody seems to perform it today.

The bag should be made of stout kraft or manilla paper, otherwise there is a danger of its being torn when the magician does what's necessary inside. It should be at least a foot longer than the performer's height, and must be wide enough for him to stoop down and touch his feet while inside it.

Besides the bag, the magician needs a needle and some strong thread, some sealing wax and a lamp to melt it, and a screen to cover him while he gets out of the bag. That's what the audience see. What they don't see is a razor blade, which the magician carries about him secretly, and a small tube of gum or rubber solution. A pair of scissors is also handy, but not essential.

To get into the bag, it's easiest to draw it over the feet while sitting on a chair. When the feet reach the bottom, the magician stands up and the bag is pulled over his head. A member of the audience then stands on the chair and runs the needle and thread in long stitches through the top of the bag, sewing the two edges together. This is better than having the top of the bag bunched up and tied, as it doesn't take anything off the height or width of the bag.

When the bag is sewn up, sealing wax is applied generously to the thread and the holes the needles have made, so that it's impossible to get out of the bag through the top. What happens, of course, is that the performer gets out through the bottom of the bag.

Once the screen is placed round the magician in the bag— and an assistant is necessary for this job, and to see that nobody peeps behind the screen—the magician stoops down and cuts a straight line along the bottom of the bag with the razor blade. He then stands upright and drawns the bag off over his head, being careful not to let the top of the bag be seen over the top of the screen. Once out, it's only a few moments' work to trim the bottom of the bag so that a new fold can be made, and gum or rubber solution is used to stick the bottom of the bag together again. Care must be taken here to make the joint exactly like the original joint.

I can vouch for the effectiveness of this escape, having used it regularly in the days when I was able to stoop down and touch my toes.

The careful reader will no doubt ask : What happens if someone thinks of sealing the *bottom* of the bag?

Not much. The magician still cuts the slit along the bottom fold, and gets out of the bag. He then takes a penknife, heats it in the flame of the lamp that was used to melt the sealing wax, and carefully slips it under the seals on the bottom fold. He trims the bottom, sticks the new fold down, and *sticks the seals on again with gum.* If plenty of sealing wax has been used, the seals lift off easily without breaking when the hot knife blade is slipped under them.

Look at the bottom of a paper bag, and you will see that the flap edge is about three-quarters of an inch above the bottom of the bag. If the seals are placed there, they won't fall foul of the cut made with the razor blade.

This escape could be made from a sack, too, but in that case the performer would have to be careful about showing the bottom of the sack after his escape. It's useful to know, if you fancy using a sack for this trick, that latex cement will stick canvas or hessian together.

To make either of these escapes more dramatic—and apparently more difficult—Houdini would be tied or manacled before being put into the bag. Sometimes, he would have the ends of the rope held outside the bag by spectators, and would still escape without the rope leaving their hands. This offers no difficulty at all, provided the tying has been supervised properly. In other words, the ropes must be tied in such a way that the performer can escape without the ends of the rope being called into play.

A good method for accomplishing this is to have the wrists tied with rope or a large handkerchief. A long rope is then threaded between the wrists, and the ends are held by a spectator. To escape, you must have a foot or so of slack in the rope held by the man from the audience. If he pulls the rope tight before you're ready it's almost impossible to get away from it. But if it's slack, all you have to do is to work the rope, with the balls of the thumbs, up between your tied hands until you can slip it over one hand. It will then pull away freely, and you are left, still with wrists tied, but free of the long rope. I used to grip the loop of this longer rope in my teeth while I escaped through the bottom of the bag, and would later hold it by placing my foot on the bag—and the loop—while I stuck the bottom of the bag together again. This ensured that the man did not drag the rope away before the climax of the trick.

Houdini never found any difficulty with rope ties. There are many which look dreadfully complicated, but which are easy enough to get out of. As a general rule, the rope should be a stiff one, such as sash cord, and plenty of it should be used. The longer the rope, the more "play" can be developed in it. Two turns round the body take up five feet or more of rope, and it's surprising how much "give" there is even in that short length. And, of course, the body can be distended considerably, by breathing in deeply (if the rope goes round the chest), inflating the stomach, enlarging the muscles of arms or legs, and discreetly holding limbs apart a little. All these measures serve to increase the length of rope used. In fact, if you give a man twenty feet of rope and ask him to tie you securely, you may well find that the rope just slides off you if you've taken advantage of the elasticity of your body.

Houdini would often frown and mutter angrily while members of the audience tied him up, as though he was worried about the impossibility of escape from his bonds. But with a little "guidance" from one of his staff, the ropes would be put on so that they looked tight, but really so that they would allow plenty of slack when the time came to get out of them.

For the magician making a speciality of escapes, there are two good rules which I have never seen explained before.

The first is : Have as many people as possible do the tying up. This means that too many cooks will spoil the broth. They will get in each other's way, and one man's knot will cancel out the next man's.

The second rule applies where a single person does the tying up. In that case, he will find it difficult to see all parts of the rope at once, and so the magician must "help" him. This is done by turning round and wrapping the rope round the body and limbs while the spectator holds the end.

It's useful, also, to have the rope tied round the body by one end at the very start. That means that when the other end is reached, the tier-up must make a slip-knot to secure it.

By far the worst rope tie to escape from is one made with a short length of soft rope. That's why Houdini and his successors used long, important-looking lengths of rope.

Some of Houdini's more spectacular escapes were made in the cause of publicity. Everybody who saw the film purporting to tell the life story of Houdini, will remember his escape from a heavily-roped chest whilst beneath the ice of the Detroit River. The film dramatised it heavily, making it appear that Houdini

heard the voice of his dying mother guide him to the hole in the
ice after he had got out of the box.

The facts are very different. Houdini's mother was not dying
at the time, but died some years later while he was crossing the
Atlantic on his way to England. He would have needed no
guidance to find the hole in the ice, because the daylight would
have illuminated it like an open window. And there would have
been little need to hold his breath for minutes on end, because
a layer of air is always found under ice.

Also, there's a rumour that Houdini had a diver standing by
beneath the water.

One of Houdini's most news-worthy photographs shows him
hanging by the heels from a jib projecting over the edge of a
skyscraper, and struggling to free himself from a strait-jacket.

I have seen the clever young magician Alan Alan make a
much more spectacular strait-jacket escape than this. Alan will
hang from a 100-foot crane, bound in a strait-jacket, while
someone sets fire to the petrol-soaked rope on which he is
suspended. Unless he's out of the strait-jacket and back up the
rope within a matter of seconds, he runs the risk of falling 100
feet when the rope burns through. Alan once failed to escape by
a fraction of a second, and was badly burned before he could be
got down to earth. That was at Battersea Park Pleasure Gardens
in London, and hundreds of people saw his near-fatal accident.

But Alan Alan survived, and is escaping from strait-jackets
while hanging upside down to this day. May he long continue
his career as a magician! But I, for one, would like to see him
adopt some less arduous livelihood.

No doubt if Houdini had had the brilliant idea of setting fire
to the rope suspending him, he'd have done it. But perhaps, on
second thoughts, he wouldn't. For Houdini, while appearing to
the public as a dare-devil performer, was really a prudent,
thoughtful man. When Harry Kellar, the famous American
magician of the turn of the century, pleaded with him to
abandon the Bullet-Catching Trick, he did so. Kellar warned
him that the trick had killed too many magicians, so Houdini
took his advice and discontinued it in his own programmes.

In many of his escapes from locked boxes and the like,
Houdini would be heavily bound before being put into the box.

Then the box would be roped and strapped up so efficiently that it seemed impossible for him to escape from his own bonds, the box, and the ropes around the box. But he could appear outside his curtained cabinet almost as soon as the box had been put inside.

The secret was a subtle one. The fact was that it took him much longer to escape from his own bonds than from the box. And so he gave the committee from the audience plenty to do by way of securing the box. This took several minutes, and those minutes allowed Houdini to get out of his own ropes and manacles, and be ready to start on the escape from the box the minute it was out of sight of the audience.

It was one of Houdini's rules that any box presented to him as a challenge should be delivered to the theatre so that he could examine it beforehand. And when he *did* escape, at the show that evening, the box would stand examination and be guaranteed as being the same box.

The reason for having the box presented at the theatre, of course, was so that he and his mechanics could prepare the box and make it escapable-from, if you will pardon the dreadful word.

There are so many ways of faking a box that it would be impossible to describe them all here. One quick and sure way was to take out some of the screws holding the box together, and replace them with dummy screws. These were only screw-heads, which did not penetrate both thicknesses of wood. They would look exactly the same as the original screws, and would be held in place by perhaps one or two turns. By pressure applied from the inside, they would be forced out and Houdini could escape. He would then sit down with a screwdriver and the original screws, and replace them tightly.

Sometimes, if any evidence of tampering with the box might show, he would rivet screws and nails over at the end, so that the box had to be destroyed to get them out.

You might think that would make a pretty loud noise. So it did. But the orchestra made an even louder noise!

Although Houdini is greatly admired by magicians all over the world, there was one of his illusions that still raises a laugh when it's mentioned. That was his famous Vanishing Elephant illusion.

Some time ago, the British Broadcasting Corporation televised a feature about Houdini, in which the Vanishing Elephant figured. In that version, an elephant was led on to the stage, the actor playing Houdini (who, incidentally, looked nothing like him) flapped his cloak at it, and the great beast vanished.

Just like that. WHOOF! And the elephant had gone.

That, of course, was a piece of camera trickery, and not a bit like the real Vanishing Elephant illusion.

What really happened was something like this: an elephant was led on to the stage, and then four stage-hands pushed on a large cage on wheels. It was shown on all sides, and then the door was opened and the elephant was led inside. Blinds were dropped, a pistol was fired, the blinds shot up again, and the cage was apparently empty. At any rate, it was wheeled off as being empty.

But whereas three or four men had wheeled the cage *on* the stage without any effort, it needed six or eight men to wheel it *off*! And even then, they had to bend their backs pretty strenuously to move it.

If you begin to suspect that the elephant was still in the cage, you'll be quite correct. And more than that I don't propose to say about the Vanishing Elephant, as other illusions are based on the same principle and are being performed today. Go and see them, and reason it out for yourself.

The year before he died—1925—Houdini did what he'd always set his mind upon. He took out a full evening's magic show and presented it in the biggest theatres. No longer was he tied to thirty or forty minutes as the top of the bill in a vaudeville show, but could take up the whole evening and present tricks and illusions apart from the escapes which had made him famous.

And Houdini was a brilliant magician, apart from his skill as The Handcuff King. Many magicians who knew him believe that he was far more expert at small magic and card work than in the illusion field. They cite his Vanishing Elephant as a dreadful example of how *not* to stage an illusion. But all are agreed that Houdini's skill as a manipulator was of the highest degree.

Some small magic shows up well on a theatre stage—but not much. One trick which Houdini showed to audiences of a thousand and more was done with a packet of needles and a reel of thread. Possibly the smallest props you could find, but Houdini made it a dramatic, stage-filling miracle. That was the East Indian Needle Trick.

In this, the magician takes a number of needles and a length of thread and apparently swallows them. He then fishes the end of the thread from his mouth, and draws it out so that it is seen that all the needles are threaded on the cotton. Houdini used to make the thread stretch the whole width of the stage, and with pin-sharp lighting against the black background, the gleaming needles could be seen swinging at three-inch intervals from the white cotton.

This has always been a most spectacular trick, and if you want to see it done perfectly today you should see Harold Holden, the well-known London magician, perform it.

Like many professional magicians, Houdini was an earnest student of everything pertaining to magic. His enormous collection of books, periodicals, pictures, programmes and playbills, all concerning magic and its allied arts, was beyond price at the time of his death. It rests today in the Library of the National Museum of New York.

For most of his life Houdini was a bitter opponent of fraudulent spiritualists, and spent much time and money in his efforts to expose them. Yet, despite his antagonism to this creed, he was a staunch friend of Sir Arthur Conan Doyle, creator of Sherlock Holmes, and one of the leaders of British spiritualism. Sir Arthur used to declare his solemn belief that Houdini could dematerialise himself and pass through solid obstacles. Thus arose one of the most prevalent and fantastic of the legends around the name of Houdini.

It may be, of course, that Sir Arthur was a little shrewder than Houdini thought, and that he expressed the dematerialisation theory so that Houdini would at last say: "No. It's not dematerialisation at all. *This* is how it's done. . . ." But Houdini, however much he may have been tempted, never told Sir Arthur Conan Doyle just how the escape tricks were performed.

It's almost impossible to expose fraudulent spiritualists, unless you catch them in the act, and are lucky enough to have disinterested witnesses. And so the best that Houdini could do, in many cases, was to duplicate their effects, and then to explain the trick of it. This often brought the answer: "Certainly Houdini can do these things by trickery, but *we* can do them by supernatural means!" Which brought still more prestige to the spiritualists, who regarded Houdini as a powerful benefactor in his way. The facts speak for themselves. Much as Houdini did to discredit the frauds, there are as many bogus spiritualistic mediums in practice today as there were thirty years ago.

Where a magician with the expert training of Houdini could witness so-called spiritualistic phenomena and at once detect the method of producing them, an ordinary person sees such demonstrations very differently. What is obvious and blatant fraud to a magician becomes sheer supernatural magic to a person unacquainted with conjuring principles.

Nevertheless, in spite of Houdini's hostility to spiritualism, he made a pact with his wife Beatrice that if he should die before she did, he would attempt to come back from the spirit world and give her evidence of survival after death. Beatrice Houdini held a seance on the anniversary of her husband's death every year for twenty-six years. But Houdini never returned to her. That's not to say that nobody else reported communications from the shade of Houdini. The Handcuff King's spirit has been a good drawing card with the fake mediums ever since he died.

But never once has a medium been able to persuade the ghostly visitor to tell one particular word. That was the password agreed upon by Houdini and his wife, and Beatrice Houdini never found a medium who could answer one question. The question was: *"What was the pet name Houdini was called by his mother in his childhood?"*

Only Beatrice Houdini, among living people, knew that name, and she is now dead. She died without evidence that Houdini lived on after death.

But she knew, as people know today, that Houdini would live on for many years as a fabulous name. Which is only fitting, for he was a fabulous man.

Chapter Ten

MARKED CARDS!

Marked cards!

The novelist—wasn't it Sabatini?—who started a book with that dramatic opening paragraph certainly knew his craft. There's a sort of disreputable, devil-may-care glamour to the very sound of the words. But the magician doesn't think them so dashing. If he's been conjuring for more than a few weeks, he's probably sick of the sound of them. The fact is, "Marked cards!" ranks with "Ah yes! Mirrors!" and "But of course, if we could have seen the threads . . ."

The public, you see, like to think that marked cards provide the card conjurer with the means of producing his miracles. And the inexperienced magician who presents the sort of card tricks that *all* inexperienced magicians inevitably present is challenged with: "Now let me see the pack!" or "But of course, that's easy with *your* cards. Now do the same trick with *my* cards!"

Alas! Marked cards are rarely used in card magic. Your good —even moderately good—conjurer usually despises them. He can get far better effects with an ordinary pack. One very good reason for this is the fact that most standard brands of marked cards with the secret markings *printed* on them are of poor quality stock. Another reason is that, in England at least, too many small boys, as well as grown-ups who should know better, own an exactly similar pack of marked cards themselves.

The wise conjurer who wishes to use marked cards will obtain his pack (and pay a high price for it) from the U.S.A., where gambling supply houses offer a much superior product. And in America, the marked card enthusiast will no doubt benefit by ordering from Great Britain, and thus get a card that isn't too familiar to American small boys.

It seems easy enough to track back on the history of marked cards. One can pretty safely say that the first gambler to notice that there was a dirty thumb-mark on the back of the Eight of Chalices was the first man to cash in on marked cards. The early playing cards had plain white backs; the pattern on the backs only came after some myopic loser was tipped off about that dirty thumb-mark. And when the patterns arrived, with them came the dishonest gambler's big chance.

For it isn't easy to mark a plain white piece of card without the mark being obvious to the other players. A slight spot inserted into a printed pattern, or a tiny gap scraped through a decorative line, can rarely be found, but a readable mark on plain card sticks out a mile.

And so the early gamblers didn't mark their cards. They took careful note of slight imperfections on the white surface. If that seems hard to believe, take a good look at the page you're reading now. Within sixty seconds, if you have reasonable eyesight, you should have found half a dozen slight imperfections in the white paper. They may be discolorations, tiny specks of foreign matter pulped into the paper, irregularities of surface, or even dirty thumb-marks!

These flaws are known as *points de repère,* and they necessarily vary from page to page. In the same way, they varied from card to card. That gave the man with sharp eyes and a good memory lots to work on. But it was working the hard way. Try memorising fifty-two different pieces of paper by the natural flaws on them. Would you like to stake money on the result? Of course not.

But take a marked pack of cards in your hands and—after you've learnt the secrets of the marking system—try again. You'll identify every card with a very few minutes' practice.

There's one way to find out whether a pack of cards carries secret markings on the back. It's not much good examining a single card; you'll need most of the pack. Take the pack in one hand and grip it firmly at one end. Then riffle the other end so that the cards flip by rapidly. Watch the pattern on the back. If the cards are unmarked, the pattern will appear to be standing still. But if a number of the cards—not necessarily all—are marked, then you'll notice a tiny spot jumping all over the place. Stop riffling the pack and look at that part of the pattern where the spot was leaping about. Compare that bit of the decoration with the same bit on the next card. There'll be a tiny discrepancy. Perhaps the stem of a flower will show a thin break in different places on different cards. Or you might see that the same flower stem has developed minute knobs in varying regions. Now this won't mean anything unless you know exactly what each break in, or addition to, the pattern signifies. The best marked cards are those marked by hand, rather than those that are printed and sold by the thousand packs. The markings on one pack are never the same as those on another in the handmade job, but the factory-produced "readers" (that's the conjurer's name, as well as the gambler's, for marked cards) can be learnt in a few seconds.

You may be surprised to learn that there are scores of ways of marking playing cards on the backs. Retouching with ink, or scraping through a portion of pattern with a needle, are the elementary methods. In the annals of card magic you may read of needled cards, edge-readers, daub-marked cards, nail nicks, dull cards, shiny cards, dusted cards, glowing cards, sanded cards, front-readers and many other types of marking systems. If you sat in a game in which almost any of these cards were in play, you'd be none the wiser. You might look for secret markings on the backs of almost any of them, and find nothing in the least suspicious.

Read, then, how easy it is to produce a pack of marked cards that is all but indetectable under examination.

First—ink-marked cards. In these days of ball-point pens, anybody could mark a pack neatly and efficiently. It wasn't always so. Before quick-drying inks came into everyday use, a special type of marking ink was sold to gamblers, which matched up in colour and surface sheen to the printing ink used by playing card manufacturers. Nowadays, ball-point pen ink does almost exactly that. It may need a brisk polish with a soft cloth after application, to bring it to the right degree of shine, but the chances are that any light mark made with a ball-pen will at once dry to the same texture as playing card printing ink.

The commonest colours used to print playing card backs are red and blue—just the colours which are most frequently used in ball-pens!

It's not sufficient to make a secret mark that's difficult for the other fellow to see. Your mark must be instantly visible—and significant—to you. Otherwise, what good is it to you?

So, to ensure this, the marking must be at the same approximate place on each card. Usually, this is the upper left-hand corner. That's because this corner is visible when cards are fanned, back outwards, in the hand.

How does the gambler or the magician make a readily readable secret mark? The easiest method is to use a clock dial system. If there's anything in the pattern that is roughly circular, he thinks of it as a clock face, and puts in his mark at the appropriate place to represent a figure. That provides twelve figures—representing the cards from Ace to Queen.

Now for the suits. He requires three markings for suits, one for, say, Clubs, one for Hearts, and one for Spades. The Diamond suit is left unmarked, just as the clock-face in the numeral marking system is left unmarked for the King.

So two marks on each card tell him, between them, all the cards from Ace to Queen and all the suits from Clubs to Spades. The one card in the pack with no markings is the King of Diamonds, because—using these arbitrary values—no Kings are marked and no Diamonds are marked.

The mark he applies need not be microscopic. A thin line an eighth of an inch long, or a spot as big as this full-stop—.—is easily seen by one in the secret, but easily lost in a confusing pattern to anyone else.

Sometimes a complete piece of the background pattern is obliterated, either by ink or by careful scraping out. And if you were to see some of the marked cards in my own collection you'd be amazed, once the system was explained to you, to think that such a large mark could go unnoticed by anyone else.

On the other hand, one of the packs I own lies at the other extreme of the scale. The marks are tiny, and are so spread out on the pattern, that to identify each one needs better eyesight than I possess. Identification of them also needs a perceptibly long pause to examine each one.

Just about the best marked pack I have was marked for me by hand by Ande Furlong, the American magician. It's a standard make of card in the United States, known as the Aviator brand. Here and there in the pattern tiny sprigs of foliage are scattered. The sprig in the top left-hand corner is the one chosen for marking. Each sprig bears an extra bud in a certain place, and each sprig has a tiny break in the linked line. The extra buds tell me the value of the card, and the breaks give the clue to the suit. These cards are marked so skilfully that, without applying the riffle test, the markings can never be spotted by anyone not in the secret. On the other hand, they are immediately obvious and instantly readable to those who know where to look.

Another pair of packs on my shelves (one red pack and one blue) are of a type well known to American conjurers and even to many American audiences. But here in England they are unknown. Thanks to that fact, I am able to use them for tricks that appear miraculous. They are clock-face marked, and the suit markings are as visible from the back as they are from the front of each card. The numerical value markings are nearly as prominent.

The gambler, usually playing poker and kindred games where only part of the pack is in use at a time, need not mark for suit as well as for value. Usually, all he wants to know is: "Which are the high value cards?" And so he marks each card from Ten to Ace with a single mark, often quite a crude mark made hurriedly. But the conjurer needs to know every card in the pack, if he's using marked cards at all, and so his is a more formidable task.

There, then, are two easily made and easily read types of marking—the clock-face and the up-and-down dotting of a line.

Al Baker, the famous American conjurer, devised another system, which was bold in the extreme. He took a curved line on the background pattern and converted it, with block-in ink, to actual figures and letters. This was done by distorting the line and adding to it so that it became the actual numeral it coded. This, however, was too bold for my liking. That may be because I have a private fear that what is obvious to me would also be obvious to the spectators. It's a fear shared by many conjurers. Those who aren't afflicted with it get away with murder. They also get away with miracles!

I was once playing cards with friends when I noticed that the whole pack was marked, and badly marked, too. But although the markings seemed to leap out and hit me in the eye, nobody else had noticed them. This was a pack of Waddington's No. One cards, which are in daily use in thousands of English homes. Round the edge, this brand of card bears a dashed line. It was this line that had received the treatment from some amateur magician—for I am sure that no gambler in his right mind would use such a system. For each Ace, a line had been ticked on to the first dash. Each Two had a mark on the second, and so on. This meant that one had to read right along the line, counting the dashes, to identify the card.

Under suspicion as the culprit was the young nephew of the household, around nine years old, who had been given the cards to play with on a wet day. I hope he reads this book, and learns that there are more efficient ways of marking cards. I also hope that' what he learns is used for conjuring, and not gambling purposes.

Ink is not used only on the backs of cards. A small dot in the right place on the edge of a card makes it an edge-reader. This system, too, was borrowed by the magician from the gambler. Edge-readers, though, have the great disadvantage of being too easily spotted by other people.

A very old gambler's trick, adopted by magicians years ago, defies detection by the eye. It consists of pricking each card with a fine-pointed needle, so that a tiny lump is raised on the back of the card. The thumb, in dealing the cards, passes over the lump and notes its position, which gives the clue to the card's identity.

The weakness in this system was overcome by Charlier, an ingenious and almost—if not quite—legendary magical expert of the nineteenth century. Charlier managed to pin-prick each card *without leaving a hole on the front of the card.*

His method was simple but painstaking. Charlier first split each card (that's not nearly as difficult as you might imagine). Then he made his pin-pricks in the *back* half, and pasted the two portions together. The result was that, although there was a raised lump on the backs, there was no corresponding hole in the front portions.

The Charlier System of marking cards was excellent when applied to a picquet pack, consisting of 32 cards only. But its use with a full pack of 52 cards would make it too complicated.

In Charlier's System two marks on each card cued the identity of the card. One was for suit and the other for value. These were duplicated at each end of the card, so that, no matter which way round the card was held, the marks were always perceptible under the thumb. The suit markings were placed along a diagonal line drawn from the top left-hand corner to the centre of the card. A pin-prick near the corner represented Spades, a bit nearer to the middle and it was Hearts, and almost at the middle of the card was the lump for Clubs. The Diamond suit was unmarked. Thus, the thumb made a short sweep from corner to centre, and noted where the lump came.

The values of the cards were noted along the top and down the right side of the card, with a single point marked away from these two tracks for the Queen. Four cards could be marked along the top of the card—Ace, King, Knave and Ten—and two spots down the right side indicated the Nine and Eight. A blank was left for the Seven of each suit.

It might be thought that pin-pricks would be an obvious device to anyone handling the cards, but this is not at all the case. The raised projections are so minute that they can easily be mistaken for a spot of grit or dust—if they are felt at all. The gambler, or the magician, of course, is expecting to find the marks, and so knows where to seek them. But the chances are that if you, an unsuspecting victim, were handed the pack to examine, you would pass them over however carefully you felt the cards.

Few conjurers use Charlier's System of card making today, partly, as I explained, because it is too complicated and unwieldy for a pack of 52 cards, and partly because the technique of card magic has vastly improved since Charlier's day. Subtlety and improved sleight-of-hand have largely replaced the need for marked cards.

But occasionally the magician, again borrowing from the gambler, uses pin-pricked cards for certain tricks. When he does, as often as not, he marks the cards while they are in actual use. And he does that with a tiny needle point mounted in a ring. When this is done it is not necessarily to identify every card in the pack, but usually to identify a single card by touch. For instance, the magician might be blindfolded thoroughly, and be unable to see anything. In such case, it's extremely useful if a card can be identified without its being seen.

There are, of course, many simpler ways of marking the card. But still some conjurers stick to the old method, which is not without risk. Perhaps that's why they stick to it.

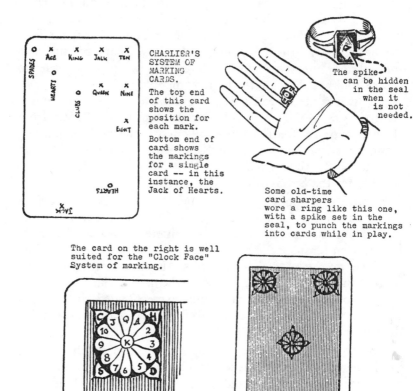

CHARLIER'S SYSTEM OF MARKING CARDS.

The top end of this card shows the position for each mark.

Bottom end of card shows the markings for a single card -- in this instance, the Jack of Hearts.

The spike can be hidden in the seal when it is not needed.

Some old-time card sharpers wore a ring like this one, with a spike set in the seal, to punch the markings into cards while in play.

The card on the right is well suited for the "Clock Face" System of marking.

This enlarged picture of the flower pattern shows the positions for marking, which is done by a dot in the appropriate place -- one for suit, one for value.

Another, and simpler, way to mark a card is literally to mark it. How many means of marking a card during the actual handling can you call to mind? Not many. Pen or pencil is out, of course, and so is any other way of touching the cards, except with the hands. So it's the hands that apply the mark. In general, this type of mark is referred to as daub, which can mean anything from solid water-colour to a slip of carbon paper.

Personally, I've never been able to understand quite why magicians should hold daub in such high repute. The purpose in using it is to identify one or two cards only. It's much easier to make a tiny nick in the card with the thumbnail or fingernail, and doesn't involve the necessity of carrying around a tin of coloured goo, or a bit of messy carbon paper.

One of the cleverest methods of marking cards is that used by many gamblers. Certain cards are dulled so that when held at an angle to the light, a distinct dull patch is seen. This is done in play—or one should say *during* play, for the crooked gambler regards his art as anything but play—by the sample expedient of wetting the thumb occasionally while dealing. The moist thumb is drawn across the card, leaving a damp smear which soon dries. And when it dries, it leaves a dull patch. As a rule, it's the high cards that are so marked. Suits don't matter a lot in the high-stake games where a dishonest gambler can make a living. Poker, for instance, depends upon the collection of sets of cards rather than the skilful playing of points. So all the cheat needs to know is how to spot the high cards in someone else's hand. Sets, such as pairs or threes of a kind, of low value cards are easily beatable, especially when one man in the game can read the backs of nearly half the pack.

The Tens, Jacks, Queens, Kings and Aces are marked with simple bold smears of saliva. The Tens might have a smear half-way across each end from left to right. Jacks might be marked from right to left, while Queens were identified by a strip of dullness down the left side. A King would then be marked down the right side, and an Ace by a smear right across the top.

I do hope you'll remember this, next time you're playing cards with that fellow who has the abominable habit of wetting his thumb every time he deals.

I don't think it's possible to produce *shiny* cards except by polishing them, but I do know that some card cheats use packs containing high cards with a high sheen on the backs, while the low cards are duller. This, however, is due to a variation in the quality of the varnish used on the cards, or in the age of the cards. Buy two identical packs of cards and use one for a few weeks. The wear and tear of dealing and shuffling will make the surface much more dull than it was when new. When this stage is reached, take out all the high cards and replace them with similar cards from the unused pack. Hold them obliquely to the light and see the difference! For that matter, just look at the edges of the cards and see the difference. The old cards will look positively black against the gleaming whiteness of the edges of the unused cards.

Although one can't get a perceptible shine on cards while they are in use, the magician can—and sometimes does—prepare his own especial brand of shine *before* use. This is done by applying tiny spots of artist's varnish here and there. Again, as in the case of inked cards, two spots serve to identify each card—one for suit and one for value. The clock-face method could be used, or the less common Charlier strip marking, where the spots are laid out horizontally or vertically instead of around some circular motif.

The weakness in using shine-spotted cards should be apparent. It calls for the right sort of lighting to show up the spots. Ink marks, on the other hand, are visible in most lights.

And the topic of light brings up a most fascinating form of card marking—fluorescent inks. I've seen advertisements for such inks and for cards prepared with them, but have never yet seen a pack prepared in this manner, nor do I know anybody who has handled such a pack. However, the system seems practicable, if risky. The advertisements tell me that these inks can't be seen by anybody who isn't wearing a special type of spectacle. So look out for those quiet types who insist on wearing tinted glasses when playing cards.

Early in this chapter I mentioned front-readers. These are perhaps the rarest form of marked cards, and are known to few magicians. Their preparation is fairly simple. All the conjurer has to do is to split the cards, pin-prick the *front* half of each in the appropriate spot, and join the portions together again. I know that many magicians reading this will not spare the time to do this job properly, and will pierce the holes right through the full thickness of the cards. But that's not such a good idea. A hole in the back of a card is much more easily seen than is any ink mark.

Whether preparing cards for the Charlier System or making front-readers, there's a special way of piercing the cards. It's not good enough just to stab a needle through the card. That will make lumps that are far too prominent. The card should be laid on a piece of soft metal, such as brass or aluminium, and the needle should be gently pressed through the card and into the metal. This way, the projection is of the very smallest, and yet can be felt distinctly.

It's not easy to trace back the history of marked cards, and it's next to impossible to say just when conjurers started using them. My guess is that a dishonest gambler first used the practice of marking the backs of cards, and within weeks, some enterprising magician had lifted the idea from the card cheat. And since then, every conjurer must at some time of his career have dabbled in the fascinations of marked cards. Few of them, however, have explored the full possibilities of using "readers."

And so, *please!*—when next a magician baffles you with a clever card trick, remember that the very last stratagem he's likely to be using will be . . . MARKED CARDS!

Chapter Eleven

THE FOUR ACES OF CARD MAGIC

In the 600 years or so since playing cards were first introduced into Europe there must have been tens of thousands of men who could, with truth, call themselves expert card conjurers. It would not be difficult to name several hundred magicians whose names would be familiar, if not to the public, then to the conjuring fraternity of today. And every one of those names could be associated with card conjuring.

But there are four names that shine brightly in the history of magic as belonging to the veritable masters of magic with the playing cards. Four names—and only one belongs to a professional performer of any note. It's doubtful whether the lay reader in Britain will recognise any of the four, but any card manipulator or student of magic will know those names as well as the lawyer knows his Blackstone, or the actor his Shakespeare.

Here, then, are the names of the Four Aces of Card Magic: Johann Nepomuk Hofzinser, Charlier, Ralph W. Hull, and Jean Hugard.

Who, but the brethren of the magic wand, knows these names today?

And yet, but for these four, it's probable that every card trick today would consist of the dreary formula: "You pick a card and I'll find it." These four men brought entertainment to the card table, as well as inventing the majority of the sleight-of-hand moves used by the magician who conjures with cards. Theirs were the brains that devised the skill that hides skill, the subtle handling of the pack, the cunning misdirection of the senses, the astonishing climaxes—but most of all, the sheer mystery of the mastery of the playing cards.

Johann Nepomuk Hofzinser was born in Vienna on July 19th, 1806. His parents were a solid, sensible Bavarian couple who had settled in the Austrian capital. They planned for their son a safe and steady career in the Civil Service, and would doubtless have been horrified if they could have foreseen that he would one day be a theatrical impresario in a small way.

Johann Hofzinser, as a boy, had some doubts about becoming a Civil Servant. Unlike most children, he developed at an early age a consuming passion for music. "I played the violin," he wrote in his diary in later years. "I appeared repeatedly in concerts, and . . . my efforts were well received everywhere."

But for a youthful fit of pique, Johann Hofzinser might have been remembered today as a musician, instead of a brilliant magical inventor and performer. "At one concert," he wrote, "I heard a boy play the violin. At first, I scarcely listened; in fact, I almost sneered. Then I paid attention to the music—and I blushed. This youngster had developed an energy, a genius, that filled me with sorrow at my own efforts, and brought me to the knowledge that I was pursuing the wrong path. I lowered my violin into the coffin, and with it, my dreams of becoming a virtuoso."

Young Hofzinser graduated from the University of Vienna with the degree of Doctor of Philosophy, and, a musical career now abandoned, entered the Austrian Civil Service. When he retired on pension, in middle age, he had reached an important position in the Tobacco Monopoly Department of the Ministry of Finance.

But by the time he had retired, he was a famous figure in Viennese Society, not as a Civil Servant, but as an entertainer in his own small theatre. It came about like this. When he said goodbye to music, young Hofzinser turned to magic as a hobby and became an ardent student of sleight-of-hand. Even so, he might be completely unknown today had it not been for a profitable sideline he pursued in the days when his Civil Service stipend was on the meagre side. Hofzinser, a scholarly young man with unbounded energy, used to review theatrical performances for the newspapers. When there was a magician at the theatre, Hofzinser was always there, and after the show would present himself at the stage door—as amateur magicians do to this day—to talk magic with the visiting conjurer.

But there was one conjurer whom he rarely had the chance of seeing—Ludwig Leopold Döbler. Young Döbler, five years older than Hofzinser, was also a Viennese, but he was a Viennese who now spent little time in his native city. His fame as a suave, charming, talented entertainer took him all over Europe. The best theatres vied with each other for his name on their posters, and so much in demand was his performance that Döbler used to boast that he would never accept a private booking, however high the fee might be. He made one exception to this rule when he performed privately for Queen Victoria and the Prince Consort at Windsor.

And so, when at last Döbler came home to perform in Vienna, Hofzinser was there to see him, and to review his performance in *Bauerle's Theaterzeitung*. Döbler, the handsome, sought-after, much-travelled man of the world, earning more in a week than Hofzinser earned in a year, struck up a firm friendship with the young Civil Servant. Döbler's showmanship, allied to Hofzinser's craftsmanship and brilliant inventive talents, undoubtedly benefited from the friendship. But the benefit experienced by Hofzinser resulted in his name being passed down the years from magician to magician, while Döbler is today only remembered by the student of magical history.

What did Döbler do? Ask a conjurer, and it's doubtful whether you'll get an answer. But ask him : What did Hofzinser do? That's a very different thing!

You'll be told that he invented the Hofzinser Pass with cards. That might not mean anything to you, if you're not a sleight-of-hand expert yourself. But if you're told that Hofzinser devised one of the modern methods of performing the famous Rising Card Trick, you're on more familiar ground. One hundred years ago, Johann Nepomuk Hofzinser sat down one evening with a pack of cards and a needle and thread, and consaructed the simplest possible apparatus for making a chosen card rise from the pack. Today, magicians often perform the trick in exactly the same way, by passing a thread through several cards, inserting duplicates of the cards to be "freely chosen" in between the threaded cards, and pulling on the end of the thread.

The inventions of Hofzinser were many. What proportion of them remain for magicians to use today is doubtful, as you will see later.

While Döbler continued on his travels around the capitals of Europe, Hofzinser stayed at home and developed the uncanny skill of his hands. He was a lucky young man, was Hofzinser. Besides being possessed of a keen, inventive brain, he was a fine entertainer, and greatly in demand at all the Viennese society functions. Furthermore, he was a strikingly handsome man of charming presence. As a professional entertainer, his fortune would have been made, had he chosen to retire from his cosy job in the Tobacco Monopoly.

But he may have possessed the added asset of caution, for he elected to stay on as a Civil Servant and work until his pension was due. At the same time, though, he simplified what could have become a complex life by opening his own theatre. Thus, his public came to him, instead of Hofzinser going out to them. It was a modest venture, this small studio of his, which he built in 1855 at No. 789, Wollzeile, Vienna. Three times a week he put on a show which he called "An Hour of Deception." It was an instant success, and the newspapers praised his entertainment almost extravagantly.

The Salle Wilhelmine Hofzinser—named after his wife—was as popular in Vienna as was Robert-Houdin's little theatre in Paris and, in later years, Maskelyne and Devant's St. George's Hall in London.

Frau Hofzinser was a model for all magicians' wives. Not only was she *interested* in her husband's magic—she took part in it! And that, let me tell you, is a pretty rare thing. The average conjurer's wife soon becomes so heartily sick of magic that she's ready to scream when she hears anyone say: "Take a card."

Wilhemine did much to make Hofzinser's studio famous. She was the beautiful lady who sat on the stage blindfolded and described in detail what members of the audience were thinking of. She was the perfect assistant and hostess, and the ideal recipient of her husband's rare secrets. If she had been otherwise, we might have known much more of Hofzinser's work and secrets today. As he grew older, Hofzinser began to think of making his will, especially after his friend Döbler died, on April 17th, 1864. When he put pen to paper,.one of the first commands he laid upon his wife was that she should destroy all his secrets and manuscripts when he died.

Death must have seemed remote to the Hofzinsers in those days of their sparkling success. Poverty was even more remote. But the sad fact is that as he aged, his popularity waned, and he became forgotten by the new generation of Viennese society. In his old age, Hofzinser had to depend upon the charity of friends for his livelihood. Says one magical historian : "Death ended his life just in time to take him out of bitter poverty."

Johann Nepomuk Hofzinser died on March 11th, 1875. Today he lies buried in the Vienna Central Cemetery.

His wife kept her promise to him, and destroyed every shred of manuscript, every drawing and diagram, and every clue to the secrets he had contrived.

How, then, may conjurers of today benefit from the skill of this striking genius of 19th century Vienna?

We owe all we know of Hofzinser's magic to another Viennese conjurer, Ottokar Fischer, who was born in Vienna on November 10th, 1873. Fischer spent a great part of his life searching for clues to the lost secrets of Hofzinser, and in 1910 disclosed all he had learned, in a book which is now a classic of the conjurer's art—*J. N. Hofzinser Kartenkünste*.

Fischer had incredible success in his lifelong search, and his book describes fully many of the tricks Hofzinser invented and performed. More important, it reveals the secrets of their performance, as well as giving the actual patter used by the Viennese master.

In England, another door was opened on Hofzinser's mysteries by Mr. S. H. Sharpe, who translated Fischer's book into English in 1931. *Hofzinser's Card Conjuring* is a scholarly work of research, besides being an invaluable handbook and guide for the sleight-of-hand student. Today, it's classed as a book rarity, and magicians look forward to the time when a new edition will be made available to them.

Many conjurers today are using Hofzinser's secrets without being in the slightest aware that their tricks are anything but modern and right up to the minute.

Among Hofzinser's tricks being performed today are the crystal ball-casket, the mirror vase, the ink vase, the floating wand, and the lantern of Diogenes. But it's in the field of playing cards that Hofzinser lives on. Many of his card tricks are feats of sleight-of-hand or mathematical calculation using an ordinary pack of cards. These he had taken from the magician's repertoire of his day and developed into smooth, slick miracles which are timely even in these swiftly moving times.

But conjurers owe their biggest debt to Hofzinser for his inventions of specially prepared cards.

It was Hofzinser, a century and more ago, who realised the extraordinary possibilities of using double-faced cards, double-backed cards, and other specially printed playing cards. The conjuring cognoscenti today will utterly bewilder and baffle you by introducing such cards into the pack. You will never suspect that such a prepared card is being used, and by the time you lay hands on the pack to examine it, the special card will have been spirited away by the magician!

The different styles of prepared card are almost without number. Double-facers and double-backers are only the elementary steps to mystery in this sphere. You may also have used against you such abnormalities of the pack as cards printed with different values at each end, cards specially smoothed or roughened—indetectably, it goes without saying!—or cards of slightly different size or thickness.

Hofzinser it was, I always believe, who not only invented such oddities, but who set conjurers a hundred years later thinking along the same lines. And in following Hofzinser's lines of thought, today's magicians have devised some truly amazing effects with specially prepared cards. New conceptions of card magic there certainly are, but many of them owe their paternity to a Viennese Civil Servant now long dead—the unforgettable Johann Nepomuk Hofzinser, whose like will never be seen again.

And now, from the cultured, respected gentleman of Vienna, let's turn to a very different personality—Charlier, the enigmatic mystery man who steps on to our stage for a mere ten or eleven years towards the end of the 19th century. Nobody knew where Charlier came from; nobody knew where he went to. *Nobody knew who he was.*

Today, there are some who say Charlier never existed—that he was a mythical character like Robert-Houdin's Torrini. But I am certain that, from about 1873 until 1884, this mysterious man lived in London and met many of the great magicians of the time. Those who knew him and vouched for his existence—after he had disappeared—included John Nevil Maskelyne, Angelo Lewis (who wrote many books on magic under the name of Professor Hoffmann), Charles Bertram (well-known Society entertainer of the '90s), and Marion H. Spielmann (famous art critic and leader of London's Jewish community). It was Bertram who left the most complete record of Charlier's career in London. But it's a sadly inadequate record, and one that's been misquoted much over the years.

Angelo Lewis introduces Charlier to the printed page, in a letter he wrote to Henry Ridgely Evans in 1909. "I first knew him in 1874," says Lewis. "His skill with cards was wonderful, but he knew nothing of any other sort of conjuring, and certainly never had a programme of any sort. . . . His chronic condition was one of poverty. I called upon him once, and once only, and found him in bed, in a side-street off the Strand, occupying a room about twelve feet by eight, which appeared to be his sitting-room, bedroom, and workshop. His work was preparing cards (bevelled, punctured, etc.), which he did with marvellous dexterity. Another speciality was designing monograms, some specimens of which I send you. When I last saw this enigmatic old man, he told me that he was preparing to visit Boulogne, France, where he had friends. I fancy that he died abroad."

Henry Ridgely Evans was only one of the magical historians who have tried to solve the mystery of Charlier—without success. A present-day magical investigator who has spent many years tracking down the Charlier legend and sifting from it the element of fact, is my friend Herbert E. Pratt, F.R.S.A., F.S.S., who is a Member of the Inner Magic Circle. In the course of his investigations and travels, Mr. Pratt has painstakingly unearthed an incredible amount of detail which throws much light on the short but spectacular history of Charlier. Mr. Pratt probably knows more than any man living about Charlier, and I am indebted to him for many unpublished pieces of information.

But whereas Mr. Pratt has specialised in the search for Charlier material, Henry Ridgely Evans's net was spread much wider. Consequently, Evans failed to find much of the data Mr. Pratt has brought to light. Nevertheless, Evans worked hard on

Charlier, corresponding with people all over the world, visiting others, and conducting long research through printed records and books.

For example, he secured from John Nevil Maskelyne a letter which supported Angelo Lewis's statement that Charlier was in London in the 1870s. "I met Charlier soon after I opened in London," wrote Maskelyne. "I paid him five guineas for a set of 32 marked cards, with the necessary instructions. . . ."

Charlier was an elusive, evasise old man. No known photograph of him exists, and no contemporary artist is known to have sketched his likeness. One solitary sketch there is to show us what he *might* have looked like, and that was made, not from a personal sitting, but from information supplied to the artist, B. F. Gribble, in 1893, nine years after Charlier had vanished.

If Charlier had a confidant in London, it was Charles Bertram, the entertainer. In Bertram's younger days, when he was plain James Bassett, landlord of the Round House tavern in London's Covent Garden, he received a visit from this macabre scarecrow of a mystery man. This is how Bertram described the meeting :—

"He came to my house . . . and introduced himself to me, saying that he had heard that I took some interest in conjuring, and that he would like to make my acquaintance. He was an old man. From his appearance he might have been anything between seventy and ninety. He had a thin, clean-shaven face, of parchment-like appearance, full of wrinkles; thin, long hair, grey and unkempt; a mouth firmly closed; long, thin, Jewish type of nose; and small piercing eyes.

"He wore an old tall silk hat, black and rather seedy looking clothes (they were a size too large for him, except the trousers, which, though baggy, were too short), and shoes which showed a little of his scrupulously white stockings above the uppers; a clean but cuffless shirt, loose, which showed his long, thin arm, terminating in very supple long, thin, fingers; and he generally wore a black tie. He had been a tall man, I should say, perhaps six feet in height, but his shoulders were slightly bent with age. . . . He spoke nine or ten languages, fluently, including English. . . . He was very aristocratic in his bearing, having at times somewhat of the style of an autocrat. At the same time, he was gentle, very deferential to ladies, always full of well-turned compliments, and very insinuating in his manner. His general greeting consisted of raising his hat, bowing profoundly, saying, while he lifted two fingers: 'I give you my blessing,' or sometimes: 'I will denounce you before the Cardinal!' This he followed up with a smile or some jocular yet appropriate remark."

This strange apparition it was, then, that confronted the young landlord of the Round House. He came many times after that, and he and Bertram (it's difficult to think of the famous Charles Bertram as James Bassett!) would sit hour after hour over card tricks, or playing ecarté—and cheating! But Charlier would never play for stakes. The object of the game was for Bertram to discover Charlier in the act of cheating. At first, it was almost impossible, so deft were his fingers and so cunning his misdirection. But as time went on, Bertram not only detected the subterfuges of the old man, but could use them himself.

Sometimes, Charlier would accept a meal, but never money or a present. Despite his seedy, tattered appearance, the old man had great pride.

From time to time he would bring with him some small gift for Bertram's wife—"some trifling little present, a monogram sketched by himself, or a tiny sachet also made by himself, and which he handed to her, with a long earnest speech, generally attributing to these little gifts some potent or mysterious property." Poor Mrs. Bertram was scared out of her wits by this tall, gaunt old man and his flamboyant speeches!

"One day," wrote Bertram, in his book, *Isn't It Wonderful?*, "after we had been chatting and comparing notes for a time, he rose from his seat, held my head between his hands, and kissed me twice on the forehead, exclaiming, with his eyes streaming with tears, 'Beelzebub! Beelzebub!' and went away without another word. I did not see him again for a week. . . ."

What an exit line for the actor that Charlier was!

When Cleopatra's Needle was being erected on the Thames Embankment, Charlier confided to Bertram that he had, with full permission from the authorities, deposited a sealed packet in the receptacle constructed for preserving records in the monument.

What was in the packet?

Charlier *said* it contained a photograph of Bertram and a parchment scroll recording the association between the young publican and the old stroller.

The old stroller. . . .

Recent investigations seem to show that that is what Charlier was—a strolling player. Not an actor in the legitimate theatre, bu something on a far more modest footing. He was, in fact, a public house entertainer in his old age, and there are records of his having toured a little round of the bars around Covent Garden, the Strand, and St. Martin's Lane.

But—a busker, speaking nine or ten languages fluently? A pub showman, who could for years baffle a skilled conjurer with his sleight-of-hand?

Yes—and *still* he was a poor old busker. But Charlier had seen better days, that's plain. And, alas! it seems equally plain that they hadn't been strictly honest days. The theory now is that Charlier had been a professional gambler, which, applied to the card table, usually means a professional cheat. His method of marking cards was unique at that time, and must have brought him many a fortune through those long, slim fingers which could read the backs of the cards by touch.

But no card cheat dare depend upon a single stratagem. Your simple-minded trickster will perhaps win a few shillings with a daring trick at the card table, but the man who earns his living by cheating must be expert—and indetectable. And so Charlier had devised a whole secret system of sleight-of-hand as applied to cheating at cards. When he used his own cards, he was sure to win. But when, far more often, he was confronted with a strange pack, he had to depend on his skilled fingers to pay for his food and lodging.

What brought this remarkable character to London at the end of his days? Nobody will ever know. And where did he go—and why?—when he suddenly vanished in August, 1884? Again, nobody knows. He *did* tell one friend of Bertram's that he was going to Naples to get married, but that seems patently absurd.

Whatever it was that took him away, Charlier knew he was leaving London. On June 16th, 1884, he wrote a letter (now in the possession of Mr. Herbert Pratt) to Mr. Marion H. Spielmann, who, besides being an eminent art critic, was an expert amateur conjurer. In his curious style, Charlier wrote: "To the Most Noble Sir Spielman—I will come on Thursday in the evening, before eight o'clock, *for the last time.* . . ."

And so, six or seven weeks later, Charlier simply vanished. Nobody knew just when he went, or where, but he was not seen again after August of that year.

Charlier left behind him no cut-and-dried tricks ready for the magician to perform, no merry quips nor made-to-measure patter. It's even doubtful whether the two sleight-of-hand moves associated with his name—the Charlier One-hand Pass and the Charlier Hay Mow Shuffle—were his own invention. And perhaps his secret system of marking playing cards with pin-pricks may have been originated by some other ingenious gambler. Such secrets are not readily revealed by their possessors, and the first man to disclose them could easily claim all credit for their invention.

But what Charlier left was something of more use to the practical conjurer: he left behind him the memory of a man who had complete mastery over playing cards. He left proof that assiduous practice could make the most difficult sleight-of-hand not only possible, but practicable and natural.

Look at it this way: Imagine that you're a man from Mars, and that for the first time in your life you're confronted with a pair of shoes, a suit of clothes, and a wristwatch. You have a rough idea as to their use, but no more than that. Could you wear the shoes, the suit and the watch, putting them on, lacing them up, doing up the buttons, winding the watch and telling the time by it? You could—in time. With nobody to guide you at first, you'd make a sorry mess of lacing up the shoes and tying the laces as other people tie them. You'd have to develop new skills to adjust the clothes, and the buttons and buttonholes would baffle you before you could manipulate them with a couple of fingers and a thumb without looking at them. The watch would be meaningless to you, and the simple actions of winding it and setting it would get you nowhere if you'd no clock to set it by.

But you—you're no man from Mars, of course (*or are you?*) —and so you think nothing of these simple everyday actions.

Shoes and laces? Absurd! Any child can attend to those! Buttons? My goodness! We've *always* had buttons! A watch? Anyone knows how to look after that!

But you're wrong, you know!

The first time you had to tie your own shoe-laces, even after seeing someone else do it for you for a long time, you didn't make a very good job of it. Buttons, too, baffled you as a child until you got the knack of them. And how long did it take you to learn to tell the time and wind a watch?

And so you're in the position of the expert sleight-of-hand manipulator in these things. They're second nature to you, because they're necessary actions you've had to learn to perform. But they wouldn't be second nature for that man from Mars. And *he* is in your position as regards the manipulation of playing cards.

This may seem an extreme argument, but the fact is that it's genuinely difficult to manipulate a pack of cards in your favour imperceptibly. There are people who earn their living (if earn is the right word!) by cheating others out of money at cards. Some few get away with it for a lifetime. But most of them are discovered and discredited within a short time.

Charlier, if he was indeed a professional cheat, seems a poor sort of model to hold up as an example. But history only records ten or eleven years of his life, and during that time he was, by all standards, a poor old man trying to earn a few coppers by showing card tricks. The incredible skill he had was grossly under-valued at a few coppers a trick, but it does go to show that old Charlier apparently preferred chronic poverty to dishonestly acquired comfort in his old age.

And his life-long application to mastering a pack of cards shows more diligence than most of us care to use today. Charlier didn't establish a new school of card manipulation, and probably didn't invent any of the sleight-of-hand he used. But 'he did inspire one young man—Charles Bertram—to efforts that brought him Royal approval for his skill shortly afterwards. He did leave behind him the proof that you could do it if you tried for long enough—and you could do it perfectly every time. He left remarkably little else, but nevertheless, his name is remem-

bered by all magicians today, even if they can't say exactly who
Charlier was. That, nobody has been able to say.

Who *was* Charlier?

There were some who said that he was a Frenchman, whose
real name was Arelier. Others put him down as Polish, Russian,
Greek, Turkish or Italian. Was he a German refugee fleeing
from the Franco-Prussian War? Was he a stateless person on the
run? Was he that mysterious conjurer, gaunt, stooping and
eccentric, who turned up in San Francisco under the name of
St. Jean?

There were some who claimed that he came from the Levant,
and that his name was Ahasuerus, as was that of the Wandering
Jew.

And some said he *was* the Wandering Jew. . . .

Just one year before old Charlier silently and inexplicably
vanished, there occurred an important event in the lives of Mr.
and Mrs. Joseph J. Hull, of Deavertown, Ohio, U.S.A. On July
5th, 1883, their first son, Ralph, was born. Six years later, young
Ralph saw a conjuring trick performed by a neighbour. That
trick—a simple vanish of a coin—started him on a lifelong
voyage of discovery in the world of magic.

At twenty he was giving entertainments in public. Two years
after that he was touring the United States as a professional
magician, a career which brought him rapid success, but which
was short-lived. In 1911, when he was 28 years old, he returned
home to help run the family business, the Star Stoneware Company and Crooksville Pottery. As sidelines, he ran radio and
paint businesses, and farmed 300 Ohio acres. In 1936 he had
the satisfaction of seeing himself named in the local newspaper,
The Crooksville Messenger, as the town's most prominent
citizen.

Ralph Hull was a typical successful American businessman,
and a family man into the bargain. A full-time job for anyone,
you might think—director and secretary of the pottery, shop-
keeper, farmer and stock breeder, and father of a family. But
somehow, Hull must have held the secret of living for more
than 24 hours a day, for his magic must have occupied him for
a great proportion of his time, apart from his business and family
interests.

When he died on May 20th, 1943, he had provided the conjurers of the whole world with a rare principle which enabled them to perform apparent impossibilities with playing cards. It was a principle that had been noted and passed by before by other magicians. Maskelyne knew of it but never investigated it. Charlier certainly knew it and used it, but without developing it. Others had seen the chance effects of it, and made but little of it.

Hull's principle is known as the Rough and Smooth Principle. More than that I am not prepared to reveal here, beyond noting down some of the incredible effects which it achieves. It's a secret which ought to remain a secret.

Apply the principle to one pack of cards, and you can show them either as normal cards, printed back and front, or as blank pieces of pasteboard, with not a vestige of a pip or any other mark on them. Shuffle the cards, cut them, flip them from hand to hand one at a time, pick off single cards at any stage—do what you will, you can make them either printed cards or blank cards, on backs and fronts, as you please.

Another of Hull's remarkable packs will change colour before your eyes. Red hearts and diamonds will become black hearts and diamonds, while black spades and clubs will change to red spades and clubs.

A third pack, while you watch its pips and court cards pass in view, will suddenly show you green dragons and purple snakes instead of clubs, hearts, spades and diamonds.

One of the most widely used of Ralph Hull's creations is a pack of 52 cards, all different without any shadow of doubt, which can be made to change to a pack composed of one card repeated throughout the pack.

Captain Trevor H. Hall, an Honorary Vice-President of the Magic Circle, is probably the world's greatest expert on Ralph Hull and his secrets. In a valuable book he has written, *The Testament of Ralph W. Hull*, Captain Hall declares that he owns ten such "transformation" packs, and describes Hull as "one who has helped to make possible the recent enormous technical advance in the science of magic, and especially the magic of cards."

Logically, there is no end to the number of variations that can be applied to playing cards, using Hull's principle. But practically, three applications of it have been adopted by conjurers as indispensable adjuncts to their art. These are the Nudist Deck, in which each card can be made to appear printed or blank, the Nu-Idea Deck, which looks like 52 different cards or 52 cards all alike, and the Brainwave Deck.

This last-named is the invention of Dai Vernon, the brilliant American magician, who took Hull's Rough and Smooth Principle and turned out a pack of cards which did one single trick—but what a trick! The cards can be shown as an ordinary pack with, say, blue backs. A spectator is invited to think of any single card in the pack, and he has a completely free choice. No matter what card he names, that card is found to be reversed in the pack. What is more, it is shown to be the only card with a red back. The magician employs no sleight of hand and no apparatus other than the cards. The cards do it all for him.

Vernon isn't the only card expert to experiment with Hull's principle. Hundreds of articles have been written in the magical Press, disclosing an equal number of tricks possible with the Rough and Smooth Principle, and not a few books have been devoted solely to it. One, in particular, would have appealed to Ralph Hull for its ingenious line of thought. That one is *Rough and Smooth Possibilities,* in which Tan Hock Chuan, a famous Chinese magician in Singapore, discusses the theory of *half-roughing.* It's a term that's meaningless to the layman, but to the conjurer it means a lot! Peter Warlock, the thoughtful English conjurer, has developed many of his baffling tricks along lines that would have been impossible without Hull's long experimentation with his principle.

The standard text-books on Hull's work are both by Captain Trevor H. Hall—*The Testament of Ralph Hull,* and *Nothing Is Impossible.* In them, Hall outlines many other conjuring techniques developed by Ralph Hull. But the one that will always be with us is that astonishingly simple, yet diabolically clever, Rough and Smooth Principle. It opened up a new and unsuspected field of magical effects and secrets, but, because of his retiring nature, Hull's name is not always associated with it.

Which is a pity, for Ralph Hull was one of the great pioneers in card conjuring.

There are many conjurers who believe that the disclosure of magical secrets in books which are available to the general public is the ruination and end of all magic. I don't believe that—obviously, or I wouldn't be writing *this* book. What's more, I can prove that it's by no means true.

In 1949 there appeared on the shelves of booksellers all over Britain a book called *The Royal Road to Card Magic*. Its cover said that it was the work of Jean Hugard and Frederick Braue. It contained lessons in performing some of the world's most baffling card tricks. The book is still on sale at almost any bookshop in the country. And those same tricks, described in detail in *The Royal Road to Card Magic*, are still mystifying and entertaining audiences everywhere. Later, there appeared side by side with it, a still more informative and encyclopedic volume—*Expert Card Technique*, by the same authors. (And, incidentally, it's amusing to note that most booksellers group this book among the textbooks on card *playing*, instead of in the sports and pastimes section, where conjuring should have its place. Do booksellers ever look inside the covers of the wares they sell?)

In these two books, Hugard and Braue have given to the world at large a vast store of entertainment, while to magicians they have given enough material to keep them busy practising and rehearsing for the rest of their lives. In a third book, edited and revised by Hugard, there comes under review the whole field of card tricks that are "self-working." This third work was *The Encyclopedia of Card Tricks*, which is *not* on sale to the public at the time of writing. Taken as a trilogy, these three books cover everything anyone needs to know about card tricks—sleight-of-hand, mathematical principles, psychology, misdirection, mechanical tricks, self-working effects, specially prepared cards, even cheating!

The brain behind these monumental works was that of Jean Hugard, the Grand Old Man of Magic. Now well past his eightieth year, Hugard lives in Brooklyn, having retired from the professional stage more than 20 years ago. Advanced in years, he is young in spirit, and his undefeatable optimism and good cheer have carried him through serious afflictions. Today, Jean Hugard is nearly blind.

But he is happy in the possession of the deepest affection from conjurers all over the world, and with their help he still continues to write copiously for their instruction.

When *The Royal Road to Card Magic* and *Expert Card Technique* had to be written (for you get the impression that Hugard *has* to write), he had the ready help of Frederick Braue. Although Braue was the width of a whole continent away, in California, the two books are models of concise writing.

Hugard edits, and writes much of the material for, a magazine called *Hugard's Magic Monthly*. In this, too, he has no lack of skilled helpers, who are eager to ensure that *H.M.M.* continues, whatever other magical magazines might suspend publication. Thanks to their efforts, with Hugard's inestimable knowledge and experience to guide them, they have made the magazine the most valuable technical publication magicians have ever had. It is now in its fifteenth year. A complete file of every issue, from Number One, Volume One, up to the current copy, makes a possession I would not part with.

The chain of events which led to Hugard's world-wide fame as a magical instructor began nearly eighty years ago in Australia.

"A small boy, creeping unwillingly to school, little dreamed that an event that morning was to chart the course of his whole life," Hugard writes. "The boy was met by a schoolmate, who offered to sell him a book. The book was Professor Hoffmann's translation of Robert-Houdin's book, *The Secrets of Magic and Conjuring*. As it happened, I—for I was that small boy—had seen my first magic show, given by Haselmayer, one of the old masters, only a week before. The title of the book seemed to promise a key to the wonders that I was still dreaming about. A bargain was soon made, and I bought the book for the enormous sum of two shillings . . . that represented pocket money for two whole weeks. . . . From that time on, my set object in life was to become a magician, and travel the world, using magic to acquire fame and fortune. This book remained my guide throughout my career. . . ."

Hugard became a professional magician in 1900, and after playing in vaudeville throughout Australia and New Zealand, assembled his own troupe. His travels took him through Australasia and the Pacific Islands, until 1916, when he landed in San Francisco. For eleven years he ran a theatre devoted solely to magic at Luna Park, besides touring the United States as a top-line performer until his retirement.

Retirement! Hugard works harder today, one imagines, than he ever worked as a touring vaudeville entertainer. Today his audience is scattered throughout the world, wherever there is a magician who reads the English language. The list of books he's written reads like a library catalogue—*Card Manipulations* (four volumes), *More Card Manipulations* (four volumes), and *Mental Magic with Cards* are only three of his many titles—but they make nine books between them. With Fred Braue, Hugard wrote another nine books—all devoted to sleight-of-hand with cards. And he's edited others, including a great part of that mammoth text-book, *Greater Magic*.

That's just a part of the work this phenomenal figure has done —since he *retired*! It comprises more than any other magical writer has produced in the whole of a working life.

If nobody else ever writes a book on conjuring with cards, the magicians of the world will have enough to keep them busy for many years, before they can say they've absorbed all Jean Hugard's instruction.

*   *   *   *

The Four Aces of Card Magic—Johann Nepomuk Hofzinser, the inventive genius of 19th century Vienna; Charlier (nobody ever knew his first name), the seedy citizen of the world who spoke ten languages and gave his gambler's fingers a lifetime's work in mastering the playing cards—Charlier, the enigmatic cosmopolitan who appeared, stayed a few years, and vanished; Ralph W. Hull, the solid businessman, whose secret life was devoted to his magic secrets; and Jean Hugard, a fine old gentleman living obscurely in Brooklyn, whose hand has set down for all time the inner secrets of magic with the cards.

If you're a conjurer, give a thought to these four when next your audience applaud you. If they're applauding one of your card tricks, part of that applause is almost certainly due to Hofzinser, Charlier, Hull or Hugard.

And if you're just an ordinary reader, not particularly interested in card tricks, but wanting to get on to the next chapter, then please accept *this* chapter as you would accept the applause of those around you in a theatre. For it's the writer's applause for the Four Aces of Card Conjuring.

Chapter Twelve

THINK OF A NUMBER

THE MAGIC of numbers, in one form or another, is probably one of the oldest forms of wizardry in the world. Wizardry as an entertainment, that is; not wizardry as a power cult. Numbers can be used to perform amazing miracles of mental magic. They can also be used as instruments in paradoxes and problems which can never be solved.

Mathematical magic, or the art of conjuring with numbers, is but one branch of its parent tree. The roots lie deep in the soil of pre-history. Indeed, the first man to be able to count beyond five may be called, with justice, the first magician, as well as the first mathematician. It seems probable that counting up to five—the number of digits on a hand—came instinctively to man the first time he had anything to count. And then one bright prehistoric day some genius discovered the fingers on the other hand. He then had something his neighbours hadn't got. He could keep check on *ten* objects instead of five. They, no doubt, floundered along in a pleasant haze, realising when they owned more than five of anything that their property totalled one hand and some over.

Then, when his secret was out, all his neighbours could count up to ten. Eleven and beyond was probably known as "Two hands and some more." Until the next genius noticed his toes. That started the tally running up to a score.

The discoverer of "the other hand," together with the man who first looked down and compared fingers with toes, deserves a place somewhere in history. If he's never had a place before, then let us salute him now, for his was a baffling magic to his neighbours.

The same principle holds good today. The person who can tell you the number of which you're thinking is no genius. He simply has a little knowledge which you may not yet have picked up. It's equally likely that you yourself have the same knowledge and have forgotten it. Could *you* extract a cube root at this moment, before reading on? If you're a grown-up person who doesn't normally work with such problems, I'd wager you couldn't *begin* to work it out. And yet you must have learnt cube roots at school. Forgotten how to do them, haven't you?

I don't blame you. Life's too full of problems already, without having to carry in one's head every mathematical formula one ever learnt. After all, if you really feel you *have* to extract a cube root, you can always find a book that tells you how to do it.

The mathematical wizard would no doubt be as hazy as you are about cube roots. But he may have something simpler. He may carry in his mind the six-figure number 142857, with which he can present some astonishing feats of magic. He may know a little about the queer habits of the figure 9, with which he will baffle you completely and utterly.

(Be patient, please! If *you* don't know about cyclic numbers such as 142857, and the 9 principle, you shall hear about them later in this book.)

The subject of mathematics itself is, and always has been, wrapped in a certain amount of mystery. Whether it's Napier's Bones or Einstein's Theory of Relativity that's being discussed, there's more or less of dense obscurity surrounding such topics.

I may be wrong, but I've often wondered whether I am the only working journalist to make regular and frequent use of a slide rule. I use it to carry out a few awkward calculations that occur many times a day in my work. My secretary, a highly intelligent young woman, thinks I'm truly a magician when I use it. She just cannot begin to understand its use and value. Her mind isn't constructed to deal with this thing. And so, whatever else she may think of her boss, she thinks he's a pretty smart wizard to get the answer to this or that problem in seconds, by sliding a bit of boxwood along another bit.

She's my audience. I've got just that tiny bit of knowledge that she hasn't got. And so I'm a wizard. That's how it works out for *all* wizards, I suppose. Certainly that applies most strongly to the mathematical variety.

And yet—when my secretary reads back to me a shorthand note she made five years ago, at a hundred-and-something words a minute, I wonder. I wonder which of us *is* the wizard.

So you see, the first stock-in-trade for any magician, mathematical, mental, or magnificent, is a little bit of knowledge the neighbours haven't got.

Sometimes, the possessor of such knowledge doesn't know how he got it or how he applies it. Later, I want to tell you something of a very great mystery indeed—the mystery of the calculating prodigies who perform astounding feats of mental arithmetic, *and don't know how they do it.*

In the meantime, stop and think for a moment about the mathematical magic that occupies so much of our leisure pursuits. If you fancy a flutter on the horses or the dogs, you back your fancy. And that's that, often to the bookmaker's credit rather than yours. But if you decide to do the thing on a more regularised scale, you start to work out form. That's where you find yourself up to the ears in permutations of one sort or another. Mathematical stuff, you see. And if you win, it's more than that—it's magic as well.

Permutations, did we say? All right. Whether you're housewife or husband, syndicate member or bob-a-weeker, you know the word if ever you've "invested" (I love the pools' promoters' terminology!) in a football pool. But do you know the odds against you?

One of my reference books* declares that, to be sure of predicting one correct line of 14 match results, you would have to fill in four and a half million lines.

That's a dismaying thought, isn't it?

So you don't intend to "invest" in football pools? But have you ever played Ludo? Chess? Draughts? Dominoes? Cribbage? Snakes and Ladders? Noughts and Crosses? These, and a thousand other fireside games, all stem from the tree that gives us "Think of a Number" magic. They're different, though, because in any game, each participant is presumed to have equal knowledge with every other player. In mathematical magic, the magician has the advantage. He knows what he knows. The spectators don't.

* *Focus on Gambling,* by E. L. Figgis (Arthur Barker, London).

At some points, the "games" branch of the tree touches the "magic" branch, most notably in card conjuring of the type that demands counting down, or totalling pips. All the games I have mentioned above have at some time been allied with conjuring. As an example, here's an absurdly simple way to beat any chess player.

The terms are that you, the chess wizard, will play any two other players, the boards to be in different rooms and you to have first move in one game. Those terms *must* be kept to.

Here's the way you win: Opponent A has first move in his game. You note his move, and go to the other room to make *the same move* on Opponent B's board. Opponent B now makes his counter-move, and you go back to Opponent A, and make B's move on that board. One opponent will beat you (if stalemates are barred) but you will beat the other opponent.

The fact is, that Opponent A is really playing Opponent B, and you have no hand in the game at all, except to move about from board to board to copy A's move on B's board and vice versa.

It may be a slightly irregular way to play chess, but it works! It also works in any game of skill where all the facts are available to both players, and where no chance element (dice throwing, for example) creeps in. Try it with Noughts and Crosses or Draughts, if Chess is beyond you.

You won't really have won by cheating—just by using your knowledge of what the other fellow is doing. If you wish to make another spectacular entry into the field of indoor sports, you might try a little cheating this time. Dominoes it's to be now.

Have a box of dominoes turned out on the table. Lay them all face down, and have them mixed up. Help to mix them, and in doing so, take away one domino secretly. Put it in your pocket for the moment. Now explain what is to be done. Any person in the room is to lay the dominoes out in a line, face up and one at a time, as would be done in a normal game of dominoes. Before a start is made, you must go outside the room so that you cannot see the face of a single domino. When the face-up line of dominoes is completed, someone is to tell you so.

Then, without entering the room, you can at once announce the numbers on the dominoes at each end of the line.

All you have to do is to take your secret domino from your pocket, look at it, and announce the pips on each end. They will correspond with the pips at each end of the line.

That's because a full set of dominoes laid out so would make a circle, with number matched to number. As you've taken away one piece of the circle, that one piece tells you the number of pips that would have been on each side of it.

When you return to the room, by the way, mix the dominoes yourself, secretly adding your stolen piece.

You will have been using two principles here: secret knowledge (the pips on the domino in your pocket), and secret access. The trick wouldn't be a success, of course, if you openly produced your stolen domino and looked at it in full view of everybody. That's why you need secret access.

So far, with two exceptions, we haven't even mentioned numbers, and yet we've been discussing and describing mathematical magic. Let's get down to that mystic number 142857. What is a cyclic number? What does it do?

A cyclic number is one which, when multiplied by certain other numbers, produces the same digits in the same order in the answer.

Try it with 142857. Multiply it by any number from 1 to 6 inclusive, and the digits 1 4 2 8 5 7 will occur in the answer.

142857	142857	142857
1	2	3
142857	285714	428571

142857	142857	142857
4	5	6
571428	714285	857142

The digits rotate upon themselves, as it were, and the figures in each answer are the same as in the original number, except that some of them have been carried to the other end of the line.

If you want to make use of this as a trick, have the digits from 1 to 9 printed on cards. Ensure that the cards bearing

1, 4, 2, 8, 5, and 7 are selected by the spectators (either by forcing the numbers 3, 6, and 9 and *not* using these, or simply by mixing them up and laying out 142857). Ask someone to throw a die, and to multiply your number—selected quite at random!—by the number uppermost on the die. Now you can either predict the answer, or "read the mind" of the person who has written it down.

There are, of course, other cyclic numbers. If you wish to make a really big job of a trick with one, have someone select a suit from a pack of cards, and lay out all the cards in that suit, face down. Jacks will count eleven, Queens twelve, and Kings thirteen.

Now write on the blackboard (and you'll need a pretty big blackboard!) this number:—

$$588,235,294,117,647.$$

Have one of the face-down cards chosen, and ask someone to multiply 588,235,294,117,647 by the number of pips on the chosen card.

The answer will be composed of the 15 digits you started with, plus a nought tacked on at the end, after the figure 7. The digits will rotate, as did the digits in the 142857 sums, and all you need to know to announce the answer is the first two figures of the answer, or the last two figures. You can then construct your whole product on those slender clues by adding the other figures to the two you know.

You can either compile a table of answers and peep at it privately, or do as I do, and let the unfortunate victim get his first two digits of the answer down. From them you know the last two figures of the answer, and can construct the whole answer. Say, for example, that a 3 of Hearts has been chosen as the multiplier:—

$$\begin{array}{r} 588,235,294,117,647 \\ 3 \\ \hline 1,764,705,882,352,941 \\ \hline \end{array}$$

All you need to know are the figures 1 and 4, which are the first two he writes down as he multiplies (reading from the right, of course). Don't forget to include the "0" in your answer. In the above example, you'll see it falls at the sixth place. Simply tack an "0" on the end of your original number, and then rotate the figures accordingly.

If a Jack (11), a Queen (12) or a King (13) have been chosen, then you must do a little quick but easy multiplication in your head to find the last two figures of the answer, like this:—

$$588,235,294,117,647$$
$$12$$

$$.\ .\ .\ .\ .\ .\ .\ .\ 94$$
$$.\ .\ .\ .\ .\ .\ .\ .\ 7$$

$$.\ .\ .\ .\ .\ .\ .\ .\ 64$$

That's all you need know—the 94, the 7 and the 64. On them you build the full answer by the method above.

Well now, that may seem a complicated sort of trick to you. So it is—far more complicated than most people would care to face. Also, it's probably too complicated for an audience to appreciate. It's the sort of trick that's best done when there's a small group who have been discussing magic. But it's not the type of thing to inflict upon an audience sitting patiently before a platform waiting to be entertained. It's mystifying, perhaps even amusing in a donnish sort of way, but I wouldn't call it entertaining.

So let's consider the simplest of all numerical tricks—the famous "Think of a Number" which baffled us so much when we were children. In case you've never met this one, we can do it here and now.

Ready? Right; then think of a number.

Double it.

Add 6.

Divide by 2.

Take away the number you first thought of.

Your answer's 3.

And if that seems as amazing to you as it did to me when I first heard it, let me put you out of your misery by telling you the way to do it.

The number 6 (in the above case) is the key to the problem. If you work through the trick again, you'll find that *half of the number you are told to add* gives you the answer. If I'd told you to add 624, the answer would have been 312.

In this case, the number 6 is the bit of knowledge the magician has. True, the victim has it as well, but if the trick is new to him, he'll be so confused with all the other instructions and calculations that he'll be apt to overlook it.

That's a child's trick—though I've found many adults who've never been taught how to work it themselves. The same principle, elaborated a little, can be made truly amazing even for quite erudite spectators.

Try the same trick this way.

Think of a number of shillings—as many as you like.

Now, in imagination, borrow the same amount from your next-door neighbour. How much have you got now? No—don't tell me. Just jot it down somewhere for reference.

I'm going to astonish you (but again, only in imagination!) by giving you 18 shillings. Add that to your total.

All this money will no doubt be very useful to you, if you have—as I have—debts to pay. So let's pay half your total sum out to your creditors. Done that?

Now you'd better think about repaying that money you borrowed from the fellow next door. Go on—pay the man the money he lent you a few minutes ago.

You have some left, of course. Where is it? In your pocket? All right. Before you take it out and count it I'll tell you much it is. It's 9 shillings. Now go ahead and count it if you don't believe me. It *is* 9 shillings, isn't it?

See? Same sum, same method of working, same principle for finding the answer: half the amount "given" to you by the magician.

But this time we've talked about money, instead of a mere number. This time, we've wrapped up the old familiar "Think of a Number" patter by making a logical story of it. And so it seems new.

Actually, it isn't new at all, but the chances are that it's new to you. Professor Hoffmann, that grand old man of magical literature, wrote it up many years ago. And more recently, Mr.

Fred Barlow, the well-known magical investigator of Birmingham, re-dressed it and included it in his fascinating book *Mental Prodigies*.

Incidentally, if the subject of mathematical magic interests you as much as it interests most intelligent people, you couldn't find a more worthwhile book than Fred Barlow's *Mental Prodigies*. If you can find a copy now (it was published in 1951) you'll have a mathematical gold mine in your hands.

Earlier in this chapter I mentioned the queer properties of the figure 9. I don't suppose mathematicians will ever exhaust all the possibilities of juggling with this digit.

Here's just one curious experiment in which the figure 9 plays the leading rôle:—

Write down any large number. It can have two, three, four or any number of digits in it.

"Scramble" those digits in any order you like.

Subtract the smaller number from the larger.

Total the digits in the answer.

Now, if your result contains two or more digits, add *those* digits. Do this until you're left with a single figure.

It's 9, isn't it?

And it always will be.

Try it out with the figures in front of you:—

Write down large number	6234972
Scramble digits	2349762

Subtract, and the answer is	3885210

Add digits in your answer ... $3+8+8+5+2+1+0=27$
Add these digits ...   ... $2+7=9$

Another odd point about that sum is that the answer is always a multiple of 9. Knowing this, you can present quite a mystifying trick. Have the sum calculated by a spectator, and then tell him to erase one figure in his answer, and to total the rest. Now he is to erase the whole sum, simply leaving on the blackboard the last total he reached. By one quick look at it, you can tell him the figure he erased from the answer. You do this simply by deducting the figure from the next highest multiple of 9.

In the example above, if the figure 3 had been erased from the answer, he'd have arrived at 24 when he totalled the digits. So you deduct 24 from the next highest multiple of 9, and are left with 3—the figure that's been rubbed out. Or, you could add 2 and 4, which would give you 6—3 less than 9.

If you delve a little more into the mystery of numbers, you'll find that the figure 9 seems to keep things in order. Most mathematical mysteries throw up the figure 9 somewhere, either as a multiple, or as the basic figure of the answer.

And if 9 is the figure that makes for harmony (only in conjuring! In other mystic arts, 9 isn't always so harmonious!) then 8 seems to be the figure that brings disorder.

If you don't believe that, try this strange sum :—

Write down the digits, *excluding* 8   12345679

Multiply by any digit, itself multiplied by 9
(say 3)   27

86419753
24691358

333333333

Try it with any of the digits multiplied by 9. You'll always get an answer composed of the same digit repeated 9 times. And the answer always adds up to a multiple of 9!

Royal Vale Heath, the American mathematician and magician, in his book *Mathemagic*, drew attention to some oddities of that row of digits which excluded the figure 8. Try, for instance, multiplying 12345679 by any multiple of 3. You'll run through some strange numerical fugues and symphonies before you've done!

But if you *include* the 8 in your original string of digits, what do you get? Just figures! So—could it be the otherwise respectable 8 which upsets our numerical scherzo? Think about it!

These experiments with figures are exceedingly interesting— if you're interested in such things! But I'm afraid it must be admitted that many people aren't interested in long calculations which only result in an unusual total. And so if you'd like to

have a really baffling and entertaining little numerical mystery,
try this :—

(a) Ask a friend to write down the year in which he was
born.

(b) Beneath that, he is to write the year of some notable
occurrence. It could be the year he fell in the river, the
year the fireworks went off under his bed—or even the
year of the last Coronation.

(c) Now he is to write down his age.

(d) Beneath that he is to write a number arrived at purely by
chance, and so you ask him to take some coins from his
pocket, lay them on the table, and count them. He writes
the number of coins underneath the rest of the sum.

(e) The last line of the sum is now to be written, and so you
tell him to calculate how many years have passed since
the notable occurrence mentioned at stage (b).

(f) Now he is to add up those five lines of figures.

But before he's even drawn the line under the sum to start
adding, you can tell him what the answer will be. And remember—at no stage have you seen the figures he's written!

If that sounds pretty baffling to you, I'm sorry to have to
disillusion you with the solution to the problem. The only item
you need to know is the number of coins he lays down on the
table. The rest of his sum is already totalled in your mind, and
you have but to add the number of coins to give him the complete answer.

Here's the working of it. But first of all, I must tell you that
lines (a) and (c) of his sum always add up to the figures in the
current year. Thus, if you were born in   ...   1938
and you add your age this year   19
                                            ——
you get the year (in which this book is
written)   1957
                                            ——
The same goes for lines (b) and (e). If the notable occurrence
took place in   1953
then it happened ...   .   4 years ago
                                                 ——
so that when you add the two, you get ...   1957
                                            ——

Now, if you add the two 1957s together, that's your basic answer. To this you add the number of coins, which he's certainly chosen at random, but which he's laid out openly for you to see! And so, with   1957

added to   1957

you get   3914
to which you add the number of coins   ...   10 (say)

and get the result 3924

I hope I needn't tell you to memorise the basic figure first. And I also hope that you won't forget to add 2 to it when next year comes round, and so on, adding 2 for each year.

Seen on paper, this problem could be broken down quite easily by a shrewd person. But when it's *spoken,* and when a person is busy writing down, thinking, adding, and being generally bothered with a request to fish in his pocket for some coins, it's almost insoluble. I can promise you this; I've used this trick many times, and I know from experience that it's a baffler.

One of the best "Think-of-a-Number" tricks is done with a pack of cards. You'll find this easy to learn if you follow the instructions with a pack of cards in your hand.

The trick needs slight preparation beforehand. You must first take the Aces from the pack. Then count nine cards off the top of the pack and lay them aside. Now place the Aces on top of the pack, and your nine cards on top of everything. You now have a pack composed of nine cards, four Aces, and the rest of the pack, reading down from the top. The cards, by the way, should be face down.

When your pack is prepared in this way, ask someone to think of a number between 10 and 20. Say: "I am going to count the cards, and when I get to your number, I want you to say "Stop!"

Count the cards slowly from hand to hand, taking the top card as "One"; the next card, "Two," is placed on top of "One," and so on. Let us say that your spectator has thought of the number 12. When he says "Stop!" you will have 12 cards in your left hand. Lay the rest of the pack down.

Take the 12 cards back in your right hand, and instruct your spectator to add up the digits in the number he has chosen. He will add 1 and 2, making 3.

Again, count the cards from right hand to left, laying them one on top of another. When you come to the third card, place it face down on the table. You will now have two face-down cards in your left hand, and nine face-down cards in your right hand, with one face-down card on the table. Place the nine cards from the right hand on top of the two cards in the left hand. Now place all eleven cards on top of the pack.

Once more, tell your spectator to think of a number between 10 and 20. Perhaps this time he will think of 19. Count the cards from right to left hand, asking him to stop you when you have reached his number.

Take the 19 cards back into the right hand, and again tell him to add the digits in his thought-of number—this time 1 and 9, giving him the total 10. Count off ten cards, laying the tenth face-down on the table with the other card lying there. You now have 9 cards in the left hand, 9 in the right hand, and two on the table. Place the right-hand cards on top of the left-hand cards, and once more replace all 18 cards on top of the pack.

This is the procedure for two more thought-of numbers. Each time, the spectator stops you when you've reached his secretly chosen number. Each time you have the digits added, and lay down the card so arrived at. Then place right-hand cards on top of left-hand cards, and all on top of pack.

At the finish you will have four cards lying face down on the table. When you turn these over, you will find that they are the four Aces.

I recommend that you practise this trick with the four Aces *face up* in the pack at first, so that you can keep track of them. If you do this, you will see that each time you make your second count—that is, adding the digits of the chosen number—you will have nine cards left in your right hand. *These will be the original nine cards from the top of the pack.* And so you see, in counting the cards twice, you restore them to their original order. And if you reckon it up, you will see that the sum of the digits in any number between 10 and 20, when deducted from that number, gives you a result of 9. Those nine cards are the nine top cards from the pack, and therefore you're left as you started—with nine cards, some Aces, and the rest of the pack.

Now this is a trick—and a very good trick indeed—which simply *must* be well practised. Before you try it on an audience, even an audience of one, you must be so sure of yourself that you do not have to stop and think for a moment. The counting procedure must be second nature, so that you appear to be giving your victim the free choice of a number without performing any magic at all. He sees you count out his number, and that's all. He must not know that you are working to a formula.

When I do this trick, I count out the first two Aces, and then put the rest of the pack in my spectator's hand, inviting him to do the rest of the trick. To reach this perfection, you must be able to follow each card mentally, without appearing to watch the person's hands as he counts. And you must, of course, be prepared to take the pack from him at the critical moments so that he cannot start again before you are ready, or botch up the counting by slipping the cards back on top of the pack too soon.

If you allow the spectator to do this part of the counting, you should ask him after your first run through whether he thinks he could do this. Then offer to show him again, to make sure that he has understood. This will leave two Aces for him to find. And believe me, he'll be staggered when he finds that he's found them!

Many card tricks, of course, depend upon some form of counting down, but I think this one is the best of all such tricks. The counting is done to a secretly thought-of number, and so you could not be expected to have any knowledge of where to place the Aces beforehand.

The field of mathematical magic is so wide that many books have been written about it. In this chapter I've tried to concentrate upon the "Think-of-a-Number" type of trick, which is the most popular. But the principles used in many tricks of this sort are so similar that we must disguise them.

One notable instance is the trick involving the imaginary sums of money. This is nothing more than the old original "Think of a Number," but it's been so well re-dressed that you'll find few people will recognise it.

The same should apply to all tricks of this sort. Instead of inviting your spectator to "Think of a Number," you should ask him, for instance, to "Imagine you're looking at a telephone. There's a number on it. Please concentrate on that number. . . ." Or else you might say: "Let's imagine that you've just been run over by a bus. I'm glad to see you're not hurt much! In fact you're well enough to sit up quickly and write down the number of the bus. Do that, will you? . . ."

See? Your victim will never recognise the old, old trick. And the numbers *you* want him to include in his sum can be passed off as "Well, the number of *my* car is 4506. Let's add that to your sum . . ." Or: "Just for fun, I want you to add my lucky number to those you've written down. My lucky number is 18. . . ."

Give some logical reason for presenting him with a number of your own. It's not sufficient to say: "Now add 18 to that."

Sometimes, when I want to introduce a number of my own, I carry that number of coins in my pocket. The rest of my money is in another pocket, so that the two lots won't get mixed. Then I ask the spectator to bring out a handful of coins. That's the number *he's* chosen freely. Now *I* have a turn, and produce "A random number of coins" from my own pocket. But of course, I already know what that "Random number" is!

Cheating? Hmm. Perhaps it is.

So shall we change the subject, and go on to another chapter?

Chapter Thirteen

THE SEALED MYSTERY

At this moment, as you read this page, you are carrying with you the world's most mysterious and marvellous piece of magical apparatus. You have it with you, yet you will never see it. It's comparatively small. Place your two fists together, and that will give you some idea of its size. It weighs a little over three pounds. It's a silent, smooth-running machine which never needs lubricating. It will last you all the days of your life.

It's your brain.

Mysterious? Certainly. Ask any biologist how it works. You'll be advised to compare it with an electric battery. You'll be told that it emits measurable currents of electricity. You'll learn that it can store up information which can be recalled by minute electrical impulses sent to it by the nerves. It does all that, and much more.

But—*how?*

That is the mystery.

Marvellous? Without any doubt it's marvellous. Who could say otherwise of a device that can show you colours and shapes; that can make you hear every sound, from the whine of a mosquito to the rumble of thunder; that can create images of events long past; that can gather, store and return to you every detail of everything you can remember?

Magical? Indeed, the brain contains within its small bulk everything that could possibly be magical, for without perception there is no magic, nor anything else. And without the brain there is no perception.

This mystery that you carry sealed within your skull is one that may never be solved. Scientists, biologists, surgeons, psychologists—all have varying theories as to how and why the brain works as it does. One discovery leads to another query; one door opened on the brain shows us another yet to open.

For hundreds of years the world has waited for the scientists to answer one question especially. It is: What is the secret of the calculating prodigies?

Now a calculating prodigy is such a rare phenomenon that only his near relatives and neighbours, besides specialising investigators, are likely to hear about him. His unusual abilities may not last more than a few years. (One hesitates to call his abilities "abnormal." They may well be normal, but latent, in all of us.)

What is a calculating prodigy?

In short, he (or she) is a person who is able to perform, mentally and rapidly, feats of mathematics which take an ordinary person many times longer to perform. Here is an example:—

Multiply 4777 by 64.

That little problem might occupy you—and your pencil and paper—for a minute. One calculating prodigy solved it in 15 seconds, by mental calculation. Could you do that?

In case it seems simple to you, and in the event of your being able to produce the answer in something approaching 15 seconds, try this one:—

Multiply 888,888,888,888,888 by itself.

If you can do that sum in 40 seconds, you are yourself a calculating prodigy, for that is the time it took Oscar Verhaeghe, a Belgian youth.

Let's consider this Belgian young man. To do so, we must travel back in time to August 10th, 1946.

At Uccle, a small industrial town near Brussels, a committee has been gathered together to question Oscar Verhaeghe. Round the table sit Mdlle. Pholien, of the Belgian Astronomical Society, Prof. Ladet, and four other eminent mathematicians, MM. Moreau, Bourgeois, Arend and Roland. Local officials and reporters whisper together while the committee frame the questions that will be asked of this surprising young man.

Who is Oscar Verhaeghe? Before them, the members of the committee have his dossier, compiled from local records. It's a simple, short document. Verhaeghe, it tells them, was born on April 16th, 1926, in the village of Bousval. He's a shy, timid youth, who can't express himself easily in words. Indeed, a report on his strange powers, published three years earlier in *Sciences Metaphysiques,* describes him as ". . . an adolescent of seventeen with the mental age of a babe of two years. . . ."

Not, one would think, the material from which great thinkers are made. But Verhaeghe's fame is already widespread, and the committee frame questions for him which would stagger a trained mathematician.

When the youth is called into the room, he is quietly asked if he will undergo the mental tests the committee have devised. He's an amiable lad, and nods eagerly.

Right. Then here's the first question: Multiply 4777 by 64. In 15 seconds comes the answer—305,728.

The answer is checked. It's correct.

Next question: Cube 689.

Within six seconds Verhaeghe has the answer—327,082,769. (Using pencil and paper, that calculation has just taken me seven minutes, in the course of which I got two wrong answers before arriving at the correct one.)

Here are some more of the questions put to Verhaeghe, with his answers:—

Give the fourth power of 1,246 (=2,410,305,930,256. Answer came in 10 seconds).

Give the 59th power of 2 (=576,460,752,303,423,488; 30 seconds).

Extract the sixth root of 24,137,585 (=17, remainder 16; 25 seconds).

Give the square of 888,888,888,888,888 (=790,123,456,790,121,876,543,209,876,544; 40 seconds).

Raise 9,999,999 to the fifth place (the answer, containing 35 figures, came in 60 seconds).

There's something terrifying in those results. Here's a backward youth, reported as having the mental age of two years, who can solve, *in his head,* mathematical problems in a few seconds—problems which would no doubt take hours to work out with pencil and paper.

How does he do it? The reports say that Verhaeghe can give no explanation of his gift, and is quite incapable of expressing himself about it. "When questioned regarding his procedure," declares Fred Barlow, author of *Mathematical Prodigies,* "he can only say, either that he does not know anything or that it simply comes to him."

Some mental calculators, however, are able to give a clue to the puzzle of : How do they do it? Jacques Inaudi, an Italian who died in 1950, and who earned his living by exhibiting his amazing mental powers of calculation, "heard" the answers to his problems, as though spoken in his own voice.

But that does not explain how the answers are reached so speedily. So far, no mathematical prodigy has been able to tell us how he is able to work out his problems so rapidly. One theory is, that the mind is literally speeded up. This, while providing a possible solution to the problem, poses another one : Why is the mind accelerated only in such calculations? Why cannot it cope equally rapidly with other decisions, decisions of everyday life, of business, of science?

Science fiction writers think they have created the type of character known as a mutant—a person whose mental and physical abilities are incredibly accentuated and developed, usually by atomic radiation. Are there such people as mutants among us today? And have these rare individuals been living among us for centuries?

Are the lightning calculators mutants?

Although each generation may throw up only isolated cases of such mental development, history has recorded dozens of examples of them over the years.

In 1702, Jedediah Buxton was born in Derbyshire. Buxton had little intelligence, and when adult was said to have the mentality of a ten-year-old child. But in spite of this, he was able to perform lengthy feats of arithmetic in his head. He had no speed, but would sometimes take months to arrive at his answer. The wonder was, though, that he could carry in his mind the almost astronomically long numbers involved. He took two-and-a-half months, for instance, to square a number of 39 digits. But his feat was none the less marvellous for that. Every calculation was done mentally, and Buxton could go about his work as a labourer and continue his calculations while working. More—he could carry on a conversation at the same time as he was working out a problem.

Although Buxton was nothing more than a yokel, and not a very bright one at that, his fame spread to London, and in 1754 he left his native village for the first and last time, to appear before the Fellows of the Royal Society. Buxton died at the age of 70, and it appeared upon investigation during his lifetime that his main asset mentally was a singularly retentive memory.

I would allow 100 per cent recall to a man who could multiply a 39-digit number by another 39-digit number!

Contemporary with Jedediah Buxton was Tom Fuller, a Negro taken to America as a slave when 14 years old. When he was 70, Fuller was able to reduce a year and a half to seconds in about two minutes. He followed this up by announcing—in one minute and a half—the exact number of seconds in 70 years, 17 days and 12 hours. He was able to point out to his examiner that the test answer to this question was wrong, as the examiner had not allowed for leap years!

Fuller could neither read nor write. Could it be that illiteracy or mental backwardness is a help to these specialised talents? Could it be that the educated man's mind is already crammed to capacity, leaving little room for fantastic abilities such as Fuller and Buxton possessed?

André Marie Ampère (1775-1836), whose name is familiar today to every user of electricity, was an exception to the rule that mathematical prodigies seem backward in other respects. Ampère numbered literature, chemistry, psychology, metaphysics, sociology and mathematics among his accomplishments. He could count at the age of three; at eleven had conquered elementary mathematics and had studied the application of algebra to geometry.

It may be that Ampère's genius for mental calculation is little known today because it was completely overshadowed by his wider and more public activities.

Zerah Colburn, born the son of a Vermont farmer in 1804, seems to have been one of the earliest lightning calculators to realise that his abilities could earn him a living. At six years of age he was giving public demonstrations in which his mental calculations left the examiners far behind as they checked the answers. At nine years old he was travelling about the U.S.A. answering in ten seconds such questions as: "How many yards in 65 miles?" or "How many seconds in 11 years?" (That latter question, by the way, was answered in *four* seconds!)

Colburn was travelling abroad and meeting the crowned heads and nobility of Europe when he was ten.

An ingenious "catch" question was put to Colburn once. He was asked to give the factors of 36,083, and replied immediately that it had no factors. One would expect a little deliberation first, but Colburn apparently knew without stopping to think that 36,083 was a prime number.

Colburn had a physical peculiarity: he possessed an extra finger on each hand, and an extra toe on each foot.

George Parker Bidder was perhaps one of Britain's best remembered mathematical wonders. He lived from 1805 to 1878, and toured the country as a boy prodigy. In time, Bidder educated himself to a high degree and became one of the leading engineers of the day.

Bidder's father, a stone-mason at Moreton Hamstead, in Devonshire, realised that he had a pretty profitable property in the boy by the time he was ten years old. At that time he started to exhibit the lad around the country, and if it had been left to Bidder senior, young George would have had little education at all. Young Bidder was just learning to write, but hadn't yet got to the stage where he could tackle figures on paper. He didn't even know the characters for all the figures. And that makes it all the more wonderful when you think that he could answer, in seconds, such questions as: "How many times does 15,228 go into the cube of 36?"

Another test question that was put to young George was: "What is the compound interest on £4,444 for 4,444 days at $4\frac{1}{2}$ per cent per annum?"

You may care to get out pencil and paper to work that one for yourself. When you've done so, I'd like to know how long it took you to get the answer, £2,434 16s. $5\frac{1}{4}$d. It took George Bidder 120 seconds.

But remember that: (1) *He did the sum in his head;* (2) *He couldn't write;* (3) *He was only ten years old.*

How does that compare with *you?*

Bidder's keen brain didn't only apply itself to mental arithmetic. While he was still a young boy, he realised that he'd have to educate himself. As a result, he achieved University degrees and academic honours in the world of engineering. If you want to see his work today, go and look at London's Victoria Docks. He built them.

Are these calculating boys isolated phenomena in their families? Nearly always they are. But in Bidder's case things were different—uncannily different. One of his brothers was an excellent mathematician and became an assurance actuary. This Bidder's talents were addressed to memorising the Bible. He was also something of a walking encyclopedia on historical matters, and could repeat every historical date he had ever been able to gather.

George Bidder's eldest son, George Parker Bidder, Junior, inherited in a high degree his father's gift for calculation, and was able to multiply a 15-digit number by another 15-digit number mentally. He claimed that his memory was a visual one, and that he *saw* the figures in his head. George Bidder, Junior, retained these talents all his life, and passed them on to *his* sons.

The nineteenth century seems to have thrown up many calculating prodigies. One Johann Martin Zacharias Dase (Hamburg, 1824-1861) completed the tables of factors and prime numbers for the seventh million and nearly to the eighth million, and could multiply large numbers mentally. One of his gifts was the ability to count incredibly rapidly. With one glance, he could total the number of a handful of peas scattered on a table, or of a flock of sheep in a field, or books in a case.

This talent suggests that some part of the brain operated to a time factor different from the rest of the brain. Could this be a clue to the problem posed by *all* mathematical geniuses?

Henri Mondeux (Tours, 1826-1862), son of a poor woodcutter, could solve simultaneous linear equations in his head, and invented processes to solve various questions ordinarily tackled by algebra.

Vito Mangiamele, a Sicilian shepherd boy born in 1827, was another otherwise ignorant child who invented his own methods of calculation, whereby he could extract cube roots of figures, running into the millions, in a matter of seconds.

Truman Henry Safford (Vermont, U.S.A., 1836-1901) was one of the many calculating boys who lost his powers in later life and reverted to normal mental powers. Safford's demonstrations must have been fascinating to watch, for they were acrobatic physically as well as mentally. *Chambers' Journal* reported him as flying out of his chair, whirling round and rolling up his eyes while he studied a mental problem. When asked to multiply one 18-digit number by another 18-digit number, "He flew round the room like a top, pulled his pantaloons over the tops of his boots, bit his hands, rolled his eyes in their sockets, sometimes smiling and talking, and then seeming to be in an agony, until, in not more than one minute, said he:—

"133,491,850,208,566,925,016,658,299,941,583,225!"

Well—wouldn't *you* be driven just as frenzied if *you* had to provide an answer like that?

Some of the mathematical prodigies have admitted that they solved their problems beforehand and memorised the answers. Cheating? Not at all. Indeed, they probably went about it the hard way by stocking their minds with an incredible mass of statistics. Ugo Zaneboni, an Italian born in 1867, demonstrated his mathematical talents on the stage. Fred Barlow reports that Zaneboni had committed to memory a vast body of statistics on which he was later questioned. He had memorised many perfect squares, cubes, etc., with their roots.

That's one way to accomplish mental miracles. But what would you make of a boy who apparently didn't have the intelligence to do that, and yet, at 16, could astound a learned society by his mental calculations? In 1912, a Singhalese youth named Arumogam did just that. He came of low-caste parents, and was immature mentally. But when asked to multiply 1,001,001 by 100,100 he was able to do so in seconds.

That was just one of the tests put to him by the Royal Asiatic Society, in Colombo. Another question was: "A wheel has a circumference of $3\frac{1}{4}$ yards. How many times will the wheel turn in travelling 26 miles?"

Arumogam answered that one, too, correctly. Which shows that he must have devised a system of his own for computing his answers, as well as being able to eliminate the extraneous details of a question.

If you or I were asked this question, we should straightway become involved with thoughts of *pi* R. squared, and lose ourselves in a welter of decimal points. Whereas Arumogam, who almost certainly did not know the key figure 3.14159, went straight to the heart of the problem and divided 26 miles by $3\frac{1}{4}$ yards. After all, when you think it over, *pi* doesn't enter into the problem at all. And Arumogam, not having heard of *pi*, would therefore not be befuddled by its uninvited intrusion into his reckonings.

What happened to Arumogam, who is almost of our own generation?

After his successful demonstrations to the Royal Asiatic Society, a Brahmin hired him from his mother for a monthly fee of 22 rupees (£2 4s.) and exhibited him in public, making large sums of money in the process. Later, Arumogam was "placed in the care of a cashier of the Madras Bank," Fred Barlow states.

As the youth had already earned himself the title of "The human ready reckoner," it is to be supposed that the clerk in question was able to expedite his own work quite usefully.

In our own century there have been four recorded cases of master-brains in the calculating field.

Edward Mills, born in Leeds in 1902, would help to gather a "pitch" for market-men by demonstrating his mental abilities as a boy. Invited to go on the music halls, Mr. Mills refused. No doubt his mental abilities extended much further than rapid figuring, for the life of a vaudeville artist is no easy one in these days of depleted engagements. Mr. Mills knew enough to keep out of a dying-on-its-feet dead-end job, for which he is no doubt truly thankful today.

In France, scientists have discussed long and learnedly the mental talents of Maurice Dagbert, who was born in Calais in 1913. But still they cannot tell how Dagbert is able to extract the cube root of 484,050,967,814,413 in 120 seconds. If you're interested, the answer is 78,517.

Mind you, Dagbert is near enough to us in time for many living witnesses of his powers to be available. And it seems to be the opinion of some of these witnesses that Dagbert had many stock systems for lightning calculations. Short cuts to his answers there may have been. *But what were they?* Dagbert will not say.

Miss Shakuntala Devi, born near Bangalore in 1920, brings us literally into the age of television. Miss Devi actually appeared in the "Picture Page" programme in 1950 and carried out lightning calculations before the TV camera.

Mr. Fred Barlow interviewed Miss Devi, who told him that her answers just "came" to her. She regards her ability as a gift of God, and will spend the 24 hours prior to a test, in contemplation of nothingness.

One of Miss Devi's tests on television was the naming of a day for which she was given the date. Fred Barlow was, I am sure, especially interested in this problem, for he himself is a veritable wizard at this "Day for any date" effect. But in his case he uses a formula which cuts down the calculations to a minimum. Mr. Barlow was good enough, some years ago, to reveal his formula to me. At first sight, it is a forbidding thing, involving several different computations, but when Mr. Barlow assured me that it could be done by anyone with normal powers of memory and retention, I had the patience to commit it to memory. And now I—even I!—can name the day for any date.

And that raises the questions: Are these calculating prodigies phenomenal? Or do they hold a secret that the layman knows nothing about?

I know that when I demonstrate the "Day for any date" effect, many spectators go away with the idea that I am a mental phenomenon. But, of course, I am far from being that. All I have is an easy way to solve the problem.

Do the calculating boys have something similar, for problems that would baffle ordinary folk? I cannot think so.

It's not logical to suppose that a youth or child—quite often remarkably backward in other subjects—could keep his secret for ever. If he had some short cut to his answers, sooner or later he would reveal its existence, either deliberately or inadvertently. And many of the learned men who have questioned these prodigies have had that fact foremost in mind. They have tried most cunningly to bring a system to light, a system that would enable *them* to get the same results. So far, to the best of my knowledge, they've found no such system.

And so we must close the chapter on a question.

G

Are the mental prodigies truly magical, in the miraculous sense, or are they ordinary people like you and me—and conjurers in general?

Or are they mutants?

Chapter Fourteen

IS IT SECOND SIGHT?

"THIS SHOW works by mental telepathy." "The Piddingtons' act is a winner—how DO they do it?"

Remember those headlines? They followed the Piddingtons' first B.B.C. broadcast in July, 1949. For weeks the whole country was divided between the "Telepathic" school, who were convinced that Sidney and Lesley Piddington were genuine mind-readers, and the "I-could-do-it-too, if-I-was-a-conjurer" group who claimed to know just how it was done.

The Piddingtons hit London like a bombshell. The radio had brought them into millions of homes. Their mind-reading act was new to the radio audience, and overnight they were an enormous success, most deservedly.

Yes, the act was new to that generation. There had been nothing comparable until then—*on the radio*. But of mind-readers who had gone before there were hundreds. The Piddingtons had revived an ancient form of entertainment, and with it had built a world-wide reputation.

Ancient? Surprisingly, yes.

In 1584, Reginald Scot, a Kentish justice, wrote the first comprehensive exposure of conjuring methods in his *Discouerie of Witchcraft*. In his account of Elizabethan conjuring, Scot mentions the secret conveyance of information to the conjurer by his confederate. "By this means," he wrote, "if you have any invention you may seem to do a hundred miracles, and to discover the secrets of a man's thoughts or words spoken far off."

In Scot's day, as for centuries later, the secret information was conveyed by the form of the confederate's question. Thus the confederate might ask: "What have I here in my hand?" when he held a knife. But "What is this I hold?" might have coded a coin.

187   G1

In those days, the code need not have been a complicated one. Audiences then must have looked upon the simplest tricks as pure magic. Thus conditioned, they'd swallow anything. But that's not so good from the magician's point of view. It tends to make him careless. Why, after all, should he and his assistant (it's a kinder word than "confederate") go to the trouble of learning a long and complex code, when the spectators are quite prepared to believe that it's all pure magic?

That, at least, is the explanation I'd offer for some of the appallingly obvious codes conjurers throughout the years have inflicted upon audiences. It took the Zancigs, the Zomahs, and the Piddingtons to lift "mind-reading" out of its deep-carved rut and make it one of the world's most baffling—and entertaining—mysteries.

About two centuries ago there seems to have come a stage when magicians decided to improve this "Second Sight," as it used to be known. Around the 1760s London appears to have experienced a small invasion of conjurers. Comus, the French magician, led the occupying forces, and in a large room in Panton Street, at Christmas, 1765, he presented his "physical, mechanical and mathematical recreations." His playbills announced a machine which enabled two persons to communicate their thoughts to each other "by an instantaneous and invisible operation."

Comus (whose name was later appropriated by other conjurers) was followed by Jonas, Boaz, and Breslaw. In their day, Jonas and Boaz created some little excitement, and each did pretty well out of magic. But Breslaw made sure of being remembered by posterity. He wrote a book. He took care, mind you, not to give away any of his tricks while he was performing as a magician, and waited until he retired before exposing the lot. *Breslaw's Last Legacy* appeared in 1784, and no doubt brought in quite a few guineas for the retired conjurer.

But although these magicians of two centuries ago had a high opinion of themselves, and described their performances in the most glowing terms on their playbills and programmes, they had little sense of the publicity value of their feats. Their powers of "thought-reading" were just another conjuring trick, and were accepted as such by the audience. Nowadays, though, as any mentalist knows from frequent experience, there are many, many people who accept such tricks as fact. They've heard of extra-sensory perception, of unconscious telepathy, of clairvoyance, and of all the other mental phenomena. And this, they think when they see a mentalist for the first time, is it. This is the extra-sensory perception I've read about. This is telepathy. This is clairvoyance.

But alas! It isn't.

It's a trick, and a very simple trick, most probably.

After which uplifting thought, we will return to Breslaw, and the year 1779, if you please.

It was in that year that Herr Breslaw (he came from Germany) announced in his programme that he would "exhibit a variety of new magical card deceptions; particularly, he will communicate the thoughts from one person to another . . ." A modest enough statement. Had he been performing today, he would no doubt have billed himself as "The Great Breslaw," and would have asked you, in letters four feet high on the hoardings, "Can the Great Breslaw Read YOUR Mind?"

It caught the public fancy, though, this "Thought Communication." Within a year or two, an Italian conjurer, the Chevalier Pinetti, had developed it to something approaching the present-day "Two-person Mental Act."

In 1784 Pinetti engaged London's Haymarket Theatre for the winter season. In heavy, bold type on his playbills, he advertised that he would, "with his consort, exhibit most wonderful, stupendous, and absolutely inimitable, mechanical, physical, and philosophical pieces, which his recent deep scrutiny in those sciences, and assiduous exertions, have enabled him to invent and construct: among which Signora Pinetti will have the special honour and satisfaction of exhibiting various experiments of new discovery, no less curious than seemingly incredible, particularly that of her being seated in one of the front boxes, with a handkerchief over her eyes, and guessing at everything imagined and proposed to her by any person in the company."

Guessing, says he!

What sparked off this eighteenth century interest in thought-reading exhibitions? Two colourful characters of the period prepared the public mind for it. The first was Giuseppe Balsamo, who preferred to be known by his more glamorous style and title of Count Alessandro di Cagliostro. The other was an Austrian physician, Friedrich Anton Mesmer.

Cagliostro was the father of all the phonies. Read the unexpurgated version of his *Memoires* and form your own opinion of that statement. If there was an odd ducat to be made out of it, he would do almost anything. Occultism he found to be one of his most profitable lines, although even he seems reluctant to admit much success in his satanic skulduggery. Nevertheless, and like so many of today's charlatans, he enjoyed a considerable reputation. But unlike most of the modern miracle merchants, the authorities caught up with him more often than he could have liked. He cooled his heels in the Bastille for quite a stretch, and ended his days as a prisoner in the fortress of San Leone, in 1795.

Mesmer was also denounced as a charlatan from time to time. His curious experiments with ladies and gentlemen lightly dressed and sitting round "magnetised" baths of water, brought upon him the attention of the Viennese police. He managed to keep a few jumps ahead of them, though, and settled in Paris in 1778, where the broader-minded ladies and gentlemen of the French capital waited upon him with interest, not to say zest.

The encyclopedia defines his theory of Mesmerism as "The theory that a subject may be reduced to a state of trance by the consciously exerted 'animal magnetism' of the operator, in which the will-power of the former is entirely subordinated."

And so, as you might expect, when Pinetti suggested that he could do things that Cagliostro only hinted at—and do them on a fully-lighted stage—the customers hurried, agog, to the box-office.

No doubt, like today's audiences, they nodded wisely to each other as Signora Pinetti defined articles shown to her partner in the audience, or answered questions whispered to the Chevalier many yards distant from her. This, they must have whispered, is it. This is Mesmerism. This is the genuine Cagliostro stuff. This is the veritable product of the Herr Doktor Mesmer, of whom we've heard so much.

But it wasn't, you know.

Again, it was a trick. But not such a simple one for the dainty Signora, seated in one of the front boxes with a handkerchief over her eyes, industriously "guessing."

It was a code. And it was a long code, designed to cover almost any article carried by a member of the audience, or pretty well any question that was likely to be asked by the earnest seekers after truth.

For something like 150 years, conjurers and their lady assistants sweated and groaned in committing to memory several hundred different forms of question, by which to code the answer to the patient lady out there in one of the front boxes, or sitting trembling on the stage. "Tell, please, quickly, quickly, what I have here!" might mean such a ridiculously simple article as a watch. Or "Is it possible, thank you, for to tell this article?" could be a handkerchief.

And in case you think this is going about it the hard way, let me tell you that those two examples are quoted from an actual code of 200 questions sold to magicians a few years ago.

It's different now. I wish I could tell you *how* different, but I mustn't.

Even a century and more ago, though, there were keen brains to devise something less obvious than the banal "Tell, please, quickly," code system.

Robert-Houdin, often called the Father of Modern Conjuring, seems to have used one of the earliest "silent" codes in demonstrations of "Second Sight" with his son, Emile. Allied to a highly trained memory on the part of each, this has never been improved upon—if we can believe what Robert-Houdin himself wrote about it.

This is how Robert-Houdin described his Second Sight act, in his *Memoires*:

"The experiment, however, to which I owed my reputation was one inspired by that fantastic god to whom Pascal attributes all the discoveries of this sublunary world: chance led me straight to the invention of *second sight*.

"My two children were playing one day in the drawing-room at a game they had invented for their own amusement. The younger had bandaged his elder brother's eyes, and made him guess the objects he touched, and when the latter happened to guess right, they changed places. This simple game suggested to me the most complicated idea that ever crossed my mind.

"Pursued by the notion, I ran and shut myself in my work-room, and was fortunately in that happy state when the mind follows easily the combinations traced by fancy. I rested my head in my hands, and, in my excitement, laid down the first principles of second sight.

"It would require a whole volume to describe the number-less combinations of this experiment; but this description, far too serious for these memoires, will find a place in a special work, which will also contain the explanation of my theatrical tricks. Still, I cannot resist the desire of cursorily explaining some of the preliminary experiments to which I had recourse before I could make the trick perfect.

"My readers will remember the experiment suggested to me formerly by the pianist's dexterity, and the strange faculty I succeeded in attaining : I could read while juggling with four balls. Thinking seriously of this, I fancied that this 'perception by appreciation' might be susceptible of equal development, if I applied its principles to the memory and the mind.

"I resolved, therefore, on making some experiments with my son Emile, and, in order to make my young assistant understand the nature of the exercise we were going to learn, I took a domino, the five-four, for instance, and laid it before him. Instead of letting him count the points of the two num-bers, I requested the boy to tell me the total at once.

" 'Nine,' he said.

"Then I added another domino, the four-three.

" 'That makes sixteen,' he said, without any hesitation.

"I stopped the first lesson here; the next day we succeeded in counting at a single glance four dominoes, the day after, six, and thus we at length were enabled to give instantaneously the product of a dozen dominoes.

"This result obtained, we applied ourselves to a far more difficult task, over which we spent a month. My son and I passed rapidly before a toy-shop, or any other displaying a variety of wares, and cast an attentive glance upon it. A few steps further on, we drew paper and pencil from our pockets, and tried which could describe the greater number of objects seen in passing. I must own that my son reached a perfection far greater than mine, for he could often write down forty objects, while I could scarce reach thirty. Often feeling vexed at this defeat, I would return to the shop and verify his statement, but he rarely made a mistake . . .

"This natural, or acquired, faculty . . . which my son and I had only gained by constant practice, was of great service in my performances, for while I was executing my tricks, I could see everything that passed around me, and thus prepare to foil any difficulties presented to me. This exercise had given me, so to speak, the power of following two ideas simultaneously, and nothing is more favourable in conjuring than to be able to think at the same time both of what you are saying and of what you are doing . . .

"This slight explanation will be sufficient to show what is the essential basis of second sight, and I will add that a secret and unnoticeable correspondence existed between my son and myself, by which I could announce to him the name, nature and bulk of objects handed me by spectators . . .

"Two months were incessantly employed in erecting the scaffolding of our tricks, and when we were quite confident of being able to contend against the difficulties of such an undertaking, we announced the first representation of second sight. On the 12th of February, 1846, I printed in the centre of my bill the following singular announcement :

" 'In this performance M. Robert-Houdin's son, who is gifted with a marvellous second sight, after his eyes have been covered with a thick bandage, will designate every object presented to him by the audience.' . . .

"The experiment of second sight, which afterwards became so fashionable, produced no effect on the first performance. I am inclined to believe that the spectators fancied themselves the dupes of accomplices . . .

"The next evening I noticed in my room several persons who had been present on the previous night, and I felt they had come a second time to assure themselves of the reality of the experiment. It seems they were convinced, for my success was complete, and amply compensated for my former disappointment.

"I especially remember a mark of singular approval with which one of my pit audience favoured me. My son had named to him several objects he offered in succession; but not feeling satisfied, my incredulous friend . . . handed me an instrument peculiar to cloth merchants, and employed to count the number of threads. Acquiescing in his wish, I said to my boy, 'What do I hold in my hand?'

" 'It is an instrument to judge the fineness of cloth, and called a thread counter.'

" 'By Jove!' my spectator said, energetically, 'it is marvellous! If I had paid ten francs to see it, I should not begrudge them!'

"From this moment, my room was much too small, and was crowded every evening. . . ."

Digressing for a moment, I'd like to tell you why William Dexter no longer goes among the audience asking for odd things for the medium to identify. It happened at Chislehurst, where Tom Osterreicher and myself were demonstrating second sight at an after-dinner entertainment of the Royal Naval Old Comrades' Association.

Osterreicher successfully identified cigarette lighters, stamp tweezers, foreign coins and the usual assorted junk that we'd been accustomed to having thrust at us. Then came a pause.

Some villain had handed me a false moustache.

The nearest thing I could code was "Comb."

Osterreicher said it was a comb.

I hurried on to the next victim. He was easy. Another cigarette lighter.

And on to the next. The same false moustache had been passed along the row.

We had that false moustache offered to us nine times. By the end of the performance we were both somewhat bemused.

And that, friends, is how the curtain was rung down on the Great Dexter's Unparalleled Demonstration of Second Sight.

Well—what would *you* have done?

Still, Robert-Houdin, too, had his moments of doubt. But he, according to his writings, was never baffled. And I'm sure he was never handed a false moustache by some roystering seafarer at Chislehurst.

Most conjurers will tell you stories of magic coming to their aid in a tight corner, Robert-Houdin, when he wrote his *Memoires* a century ago, included many such stories in the book. Incredible as some of them are, the chances are that they were true.

On one occasion the famous French magician was involved in an argument with a Belgian Customs official. The *douanier* at the frontier was demanding heavy duty on Robert-Houdin's baggage. Robert-Houdin claimed that, as the trunks full of apparatus were personal equipment, he was exempt from paying duty. The argument hinged on whether or not Robert-Houdin was indeed a conjurer. As proof, the magician staged an impromptu demonstration of second sight.

The boy Emile was playing in the road some distance away, but had kept a sharp eye on Papa, who was doing a little hurried pocket-picking, with the Customs official as the victim.

"Emile!" called Robert-Houdin, "Can you tell us what this gentleman has in his pocket?"

"Certainly," replied the polite lad. "He has a blue striped handkerchief . . . a green morocco spectacle case, without the spectacles . . . and a piece of sugar which the gentleman saved from his coffee."

The conjurer had signalled these items to his son by the silent code they had been using on the stage.

Mind you, Robert-Houdin never revealed, in his *Memoires* or elsewhere, that he used a silent code, and it's generally accepted that Robert Heller first introduced this baffling mystery to the public in New York in 1864. But read Robert-Houdin's *Memoires* for yourself—you ought to read the book, anyway, if you're sufficiently interested in magic to be reading *this* book. When you've read Robert-Houdin's accounts of his Second Sight trick, try to find some *other* explanation for it. A silent code is the only means by which he could have produced the effects he claimed to have produced.

While Robert-Houdin, to my mind, deserves the credit for the silent code system, Heller has one great claim to fame—he brought glamour to the Second Sight mystery. Languishing voluptuously on a sofa on the stage was Haidee, his eye-worthy

lady assistant. And while Heller prowled round the audience
having articles thrust upon him for identification and being
invited to answer the most complex domestic questions, Haidee
reclined mysteriously on the sofa, her head resting sideways upon
the cushioned horsehair.

She didn't pose like this entirely for effect, but because if she
hadn't kept her ear to the sofa she wouldn't have heard the
messages being telegraphed to her by backstage assistants. Yes,
ladies and gentlemen, Heller used the electric telegraph, and the
fair Haidee was no mean reader of a buzzer.

Heller, crafty old prestidigitator that he was, didn't only make
use of a spark coil transmitter. He also used the more conven-
tional spoken code, and just to throw the amateur magicians off
the scent, he'd signal several times by his silent code.

What is this silent code which has been so provocatively
mentioned in the last page or so?

There are many silent codes. Some I'd never dream of
explaining in print. But the most usual one has been done so
often—and often so badly—that I'm surprised at you for wanting to know what a silent code is. But you may never have
witnessed one. If you'd seen some of the worse ones, you'd need
no explanation.

Broadly, the silent code in this form depends on the performer
in the audience signalling to the performer on the stage by a
sort of semaphore system. Not so energetic, perhaps, as the
semaphore you may have learned as a Boy Scout, but still a
semaphore system.

A turn of the head to the left may mean "Black." To the
right, "White." Left arm hanging straight down could be "Yes."
Right arm straight down—"No." If you imagine, say, four head
movements, four movements with each arm, four different
stances, and four different methods of turning the body, you'll
realise that these can convey twenty signals. Combine head, arm,
stance and turning movements, and you have an enormously
extended system of signalling.

But that's not the efficient way to work a silent code. The
smart magician does it more easily than that. He'll stick to, say,
his twenty single signals without combining them. That way, the
"medium" on the stage has a much simpler task. After all, the

magician *knows* what he's signalling, and so it's easier for him to translate the article into a signal than for his "medium" to translate a signal into an article.

How, then, can the magician code perhaps 200 or 300 articles, only using a score or so of signals? The answer is that he and his assistant have broken down the list of 200 or 300 articles into ten or fifteen sub-classifications. Thus, signal number one will tell the "medium" that the magician has been handed an article in sub-list number one. The next signal the magician gives, places the article in its correct order in the sub-list.

Let's say that you and I are going to work on a list of 200 objects likely to be carried in a man's pockets or a woman's handbag. First of all, we'll break it down to ten headings. Heading number one shall be money. Here's a specimen sub-list :—

1. Five Pound Note.	11. Shilling.
2. Pound Note.	12. Sixpence.
3. Ten Shilling Note.	13. Threepenny Piece (new).
4. Five Pound Gold Piece.	14. Threepenny Piece (old).
5. Golden Sovereign.	15. Penny.
6. Half Sovereign.	16. Halfpenny.
7. Five-shilling Piece.	17. Farthing.
8. Double Florin.	18. Foreign Coin.
9. Half-crown.	19. Foreign Note.
10. Florin.	20. "Special" Money.

Item 20 would be such things as Maundy Money, antique money, materials used as money in foreign countries (e.g. cowrie shells, knotted cord, silver rings, etc.). This signal for "Money— 20" would have to be followed by a further signal defining the object more closely.

Now let's compile a list of "Things concerned with money." This would be list number two, and might go something like this :—

1. Wallet (leather).	8. Bill.
2. Wallet (plastic).	9. Postal Order.
3. Purse (leather).	10. Money Order.
4. Purse (metal).	11. Stamp (British).
5. Purse (plastic).	12. Stamp (foreign).
6. Cheque Book.	13. Voucher.
7. Receipt.	14. Bonds.

15. Credit Note.   18. Cash Token.
16. Debit Note.   19. Counterfeit Money.
17. Cash Certificate.   20. Wages Slip.

With these two lists we've got 40 items, each of which can be coded by two signals—one to show which group we're coding, and one for the article in that group. Thus, a cheque book would be coded by signal number 2, followed by signal number 6. Phew! Forty items to memorise! That's quite a task! But save your brow-mopping for later. We've got 160 other items to memorise yet!

When we've listed every one of 200 objects, we've got to prepare another list or so. These will be the classifying lists and may be shorter. For example, what if we're handed a Swiss 10-franc piece to identify? We've got a code number for a foreign coin, but is it enough to announce baldly, "It's a foreign coin"? Not on your clairvoyant life it isn't. We've got to get the all-agog spectators off the edge of their plush seats and make them relax by telling them that this article is a foreign coin, a silver coin, a coin worth ten francs, a coin from Switzerland, a coin bearing the date 1924.

How?

Friend, you're now beginning to learn that this Second Sight game isn't such a game after all. It's sheer hard work. Because you've now got to learn a list of nationalities, a list of metals, a list of values, and a list of dates. On top of that, and just in case this wretched 10-franc piece is hanging on a lady's bracelet as a memento of the year she went on a Conducted Tour of Switzerland's Glorious Lakes—Make New Friends And See The World! —on top of that, you have to learn a list of the *uses* of money, and another one defining a hole in the coin.

Is it worth it?

Well, if you're prepared to demonstrate your psychic powers round the Old Folks' Homes for a year or two at a fee of bus fares and a meat tea, it might be. After you've graduated from the Darby and Joan Clubs and the R.S.P.C.A. Gymkhanas and worked your way into the Swimming Club Annual Dinners or the Grand Select Dances Complete with Cabaret, you'll have your eyes on the Masonic Banquets at the Connaught Rooms or the Christmas Season booking in the Palm Court at the Hotel Magnifico.

And then you'll go for television. With luck, you'll be booked for an audition, and what will the producer tell you? "Nobody will believe it's not stooged," he'll say. "Second sight on TV is *out*. Now if only you had a new angle on it like the Piddingtons had. . . ."

See?

All that work. Two hundred articles listed and learned. Another hundred or so classifying lists committed to memory. The hard grind round the Old Folks' Homes, the garden parties, the annual dinners, the Masonics, the Palm Courts. And then the TV man says nobody will believe the act isn't stooged.

Still, you can always tell your friends that the producer said it was unbelievable.

You think that's a pessimistic picture? Ask the boys and girls, the magic fans with the zest and enthusiasm for their hobby, who've tried it. They'll tell you it's true enough. But they'll also tell you that they love doing these little shows, and that their audiences love seeing them perform. It'll be true, too.

But success? Your name a household word like the Piddingtons'? Billing in the *Radio Times*? Letters to the newspapers about you? "Is telepathy practicable, or is it a trick?"

No.

Not unless—as the man told you—you have a new angle on Second Sight.

Your angle may be sheer speed in performance. I know one first-rate telepathic act which is never short of top-class bookings. Speed and wit is their angle. The man working in the audience can signal several articles at once, leaving his partner to unravel all his signals in a breath. Their code is incredibly extensive. Both have charm, personality, and a lightning wit. Theirs is not only a mystery, but a breathless entertainment.

But the years they've spent on perfecting their code! They've lived with it, day and night, practising, rehearsing, polishing, performing it at mealtimes, in the street, on the bus.

Could you do that?

All right. You could—and would.

But what about your partner?

Will she spend years watching every flick of your left hand, listening to you ask: "Very well. What's the value of the coin?" If she'll do that, she's a treasure and a prize beyond value.

The Zancigs were the leaders of the host of magicians who presented the Second Sight act earlier in this century. For years after they retired, their name was a world-wide synonym for telepathic powers. And that's odd, because more than once their system was exposed in the popular press of the day. Julius Zancig himself sold a version of it to *Answers,* a popular light type of weekly magazine. I have a feeling that he and his wife were already operating another system by then, in which case his "exposure" would result in crowds filling the theatre just to show that they knew how he did it. And I can imagine their befuddlement when they found that they *still* couldn't fathom the Zancigs' secret!

Mind you, Julius Zancig and his wife didn't belong to the "Come, tell, what have I here?" school of clairvoyants. They had their new angle, too. Their speciality was the answering of questions. That, you may think, would be impossible to do, however clever the code might be. But don't you believe it! The question-answering game is easier, if anything, than the identification of objects.

And, what's more, the answers given can rarely be checked at the time. I know from experience that when a trusting member of the audience is invited to ask a question, she (it's nearly always a she) will want to know something about the future. And so she must be content to wait for the future to see whether the answer is correct. If it is—fine! She'll come again to see the show. If the answer's wrong—too bad! And she'll most likely forget the whole thing.

The fact is that we are all more prone to remember the positive things of life than the negative. The very fact that the "telepathist" hit the nail on the head makes it stick in our mind (the fact, not the nail). Whereas a failure causes us to think, "Well, there may have been a change of circumstances. If things had remained as they were, then undoubtedly what the man said would have come to pass *now.*"

If you don't believe this, I suggest that you learn a simple trick with cards, dice or coins, and give it a fortune-telling twist.

Now try out your trick on some stranger (these things never seem to work with our intimates, alas!) and watch the reaction. You'll find that the stranger will agree with you heartily over slightly more than half you've told her. And she'll remember these things and remind you of them at a future date. But what of the misses, as against the hits? I challenge you to succeed in making her remember them! When you repeat them to her, she'll have to think for a long time to call them to mind.

She'll have forgotten the failures.

I've had more fun—and built up quite an undeserved reputation!—with these little fortune-telling tricks than with any others. If you're interested, and wonder how to go about applying the necessary occult twist to the trick, I commend to you a little book called *Forbidden Wisdom,* written by the late Howard Albright. But don't go to a bookshop for it. They'll never have heard of it. Go to a magic shop. If you're lucky, you'll buy pounds' and pounds' worth of magical fun for five shillings.

The range of questions covered by the Zancigs' code was enormous. I doubt whether they ever put them on paper or confided the whole lot to any living soul, and so you'll never see an authentic and full list of them. Many magic books carry what purports to be the Zancig code, but it's nothing like complete. One of the books on my shelves—*The Life and Mysteries of Dr. Q.*—gives a paltry 99 questions which it refers to as the Zancig code. If this was extended ten times it might be something like the full code. But 99!

This is the way the Zancigs went about it. Each question was memorised and allotted a number. Commonly used words, also, were allotted a number. Ten gestures were allotted numbers. Ten different stances had numbers. Imagine that 999 questions were covered. Three digits were needed to convey nearly all these. Right—a word, a gesture, a stance, each representing a digit, signalled the full number. Or three words. Or three gestures.

What could be fairer?

But it wasn't quite as simple as that. Take any 999 questions —go on! Take 'em! It'll take you a long, long time to *compose* 999 questions! But when you've composed them, just switch the subject of Question Number One with that of Question Number

Two. And after a little thought you'll realise that each question could apply to many subjects, or people.

If Question Number One is : "Shall I pass the examination?" exchange the "I" for every conceivable other person. You're involved with sons, daughters, aunts, uncles, neighbours, sweethearts, husbands, wives, and so on without number, almost.

That's quite a problem. And the answer to it rather complicates our simple numbering of the questions. In other words, an additional coding element must be introduced. And so, if you want to code Question Number One, you signal : "Pass examination?—Son." Or "Will husband pass examination?" So for Question Number One, you must tack on another code signal to cover all the possible people who might be sitting for an examination.

Difficult? Of course it's difficult. But it's possible, and it must be done. So Question Number One becomes two signals to be coded, and the "medium" will remember them as "Pass examination?" and "Son."

You're still determined to perform the Second Sight Act? Well —go ahead and do it. Just allot ten digits to ten simple words, ten easy gestures, ten different stances. Now compose your list of likely questions and memorise their numbers. Come back in a year and tell me that you and your partner have done all this. What happens then? I'll have bought a miniature walkie-talkie radio set, and will be coding all my questions in plain English, through a throat microphone, to my lady assistant who sits comfortably with a deaf aid ear plug in her ear and a tiny receiving set strapped to her leg.

At least—I'd have done that if I wanted to present the Second Sight Act. But I don't. Not any longer. I had a year or two working it, and that was enough. You see, people began to take it seriously. I was invited, even, to contact relatives who had "passed beyond the veil." And that put me off.

Though I still think it's excellent and mystifying entertainment.

Naturally, in these days of radio, television, and electronic brains, people begin to suspect concealed radio sets, and that, too, is a stumbling block. Especially when the honest magician *doesn't* use a walkie-talkie.

When the Piddingtons were at the height of their fame in this country, I often heard people airily switch off the radio when they'd heard the Piddingtons' act, and say "Walkie-talkie."

Now that was being pretty hard on two clever entertainers, because I know for sure that they did not use radio. I don't propose to disclose their secret, or even hint at it. But I'd like to set you guessing by telling you that their secret was far, far simpler and cheaper than radio.

What amused the Piddingtons was the series of wild and woolly guesses made at their act by the newspapers. Even quite well-known columnists made the most absurd guesses, prompted by eager—and jealous—magicians who thought they knew just how Sidney and Lesley read each other's minds. And if those zealous conjurers who rushed into print with "solutions" to the Piddington act had only read their elementary conjuring books they, too, would have been able to stage a performance similar to that of the Piddingtons—if they'd had the entertaining ability to put it over.

I can promise you that the Piddingtons used nothing that was concealed from the audience. The people sitting in the theatre saw everything—*everything*. They heard everything. They followed with their eyes and ears the whole of the mysterious procedure—and never saw it, neither did they hear it. They were looking and listening for the wrong thing.

But that's the way it goes. And conjurers are glad of it.

I don't think either of the Piddingtons would mind my revealing the fact that Lesley has an astonishingly retentive memory. So she should have, having earned her living as an actress. And that memory was called into play in many of their feats. Without it, the mystery could not have been accomplished.

Sidney had one of the keenest brains you could wish for. He could work out a method of presentation in a few moments, and would follow that at once by applying exactly the right principle for achieving the result he wanted.

And always, it was the simplest and most direct way of performing the trick that he produced.

No. If you ever thought you'd found the Piddingtons' system, you were foxed a moment later, because rarely did they use the same system in any two items. That's the way a good magician goes to work. And it's only the *good* magicians that are remembered. Which is a merciful dispensation of Providence, because, goodness knows, there are so many, many bad ones.

I wish I had room to discuss more of the great Second Sight Acts, for it's a fascinating subject. But there it is. We've had to leave out the Zomahs—possibly the most staggeringly baffling Second Sight act of them all—the Devants, the Trees, the Svengalis. We've not even mentioned Anderson, the Wizard of the North, "The Holland Maid," Young Master McKean (eight years old when he showed his prowess in London in 1831), "The Wonderful Double-sighted Phaenomenon," "The Mysterious Lady," Robin, the Herrmanns, the Fays, the Marriotts.

In a long, long procession they extend back far into the years, possibly much farther than those days 200 years ago when Londoners flocked to the Panton Street Rooms to see and marvel at Comus. And who knows? At some stage in that long procession there might have been an individual who really *could* read minds.

And—how do you know that the last thought-reader *you* saw wasn't authentic? After all, a true telepathist would never admit his powers publicly.

He daren't.